ICU TO MARATHON

diaries of a nearly dead man

DAVID JOHNDROW

Published by David Johndrow

COVER PHOTO BY CAPSTONE PHOTOGRAPHY WWW.CAPSTONEPHOTO.COM
BACK COVER PHOTO BY SARAH J. THORNINGTON-CERICOLA, WWW.THESTUDIOBYTHESEA.COM

Photo by: Capstone

First Printing, 2013

Published by
David Johndrow
Post Office Box 6544, Holliston, MA, USA 01746
www.ICU2Marathon.com

ISBN: 978-1494403928

CreateSpace ISBN: 1494403927

Disclaimer:

This book contains a myriad of factual information, which is in fact what you paid for. It will be up to you and your physician, to determine the best application for the factual and non-factual information contained within the pages of this volume; hereinafter entitled "the book". The book is the sum total of all complete, partially complete and somewhat complete facts along with a significant percentage of total fabrications; which shall further be known as non-factual information, hereinafter "BS".

The book was written exclusively for entertainment purposes, and therefore should be considered dangerous without the consultation of a real life doctor; the very same ones that legally probe your various body cavities for unreasonable sums of money. They should be well aware of the BS surrounding running, weight loss and sexual behavior. It will be their job to inform you what claims are factual and which ones are purely BS – it will be very hard to tell on your own.

The authors make no claims, guarantees, warranties, or any other legal mumbo-jumbo, for which you can hold them accountable in any court of law. We would like to warn you that contents may have settled during shipment. Any characters with a resemblance to persons living or dead, is purely coincidental. For an unlimited time only, this is not void where prohibited, taxed, or otherwise restricted.

Remember, fitness is a lifestyle most of us suck at. However, as time progresses and research is done, we may in fact find that sitting on the couch eating bonbons while sipping champagne and watching The Furor on television, is the healthiest lifestyle of them all.

And finally, ~~swim at your own risk!~~ don't be stupid!

Dedication

In writing this volume, I have relived much of my journey to this day. As I write this dedication by candlelight in front of the fire, I recall all of the souls who have been an integral part of that journey. They (whoever "they" are) say that we are the culmination of our life's experience; we are today the result of where we've been all of our yesterdays. That may well be true, but I'd like to add to that, the ideal that we are (and, perhaps, even more poignantly), a result of the souls who have crossed our paths, and helped to shape us in one way, or another. So, I'd like to take this opportunity to dedicate this work to everyone who has joined me on this amazing journey from the I.C.U. to finishing my first marathon.

I couldn't begin to express my thanks without first extending my gratitude to all the unnamed doctors and nurses who saved my life at Leonard Morse Hospital in Framingham, Massachusetts, and especially to Dr. Christopher Gange of the Framingham Heart Center.

I am indebted to my trainers at the Metrowest YMCA, my friends on MyFitnessPal.com and members of the Favorite Run Community, Idiots Running Club, and the Pathetic Runner Group, who have encouraged me to make the sacrifices to keep on going, to do one more, and to run another mile.

There are countless runners (so many of which I will never know their names) that I have met at the starting lines of dozens of races, at my favorite running store, and all of the race marshals and volunteers who clapped for me, high-fived me and tried not to laugh at me as I plodded past them. Thank you!

To Tom, Lori, Brian and Tommy because you inspire me to be better (read: smoke me at every race)!

I want to extend a special thanks to my running bud Scott, whom the cosmos has brought into my life. Thanks for your music, your patience, paying for Dunkin' Donuts, for running my pace just so we could hang out, and forever being in a different age group, so we never have to compete against each other.

But this book is most importantly dedicated to my loving wife, Mary Anne, and to my three lovely daughters, who would like to eat dinner without a caloric evaluation, who never want to hear jokes about fartleks, or hear the word "running" spoken in the house ever again.

And no dedication would be complete without expressing the heart-felt gratitude I have for a loving God who touched me and led me through this roller-coaster ride called life; I call him Jesus.

— David Johndrow

Table of Contents

Foreword

This book is a true story about a good friend of mine who almost died a few years ago due to a viral infection which attacked his heart. You will not only learn of his recovery, but also of his journey to healing in the short time since then and his new and healthy lifestyle.

The first time I met David, I liked him and knew he was an incredible individual with a destiny of greatness. As we got to know one other through some lengthy conversations, I discovered that in many ways, we were alike. It became obvious that our strengths could be combined to result in some positive changes for both of us, so we began to assist each other on our respective journeys.

The shocking news of his heart failure hit me hard, but left me with a strange feeling that, nevertheless, everything would be fine. When I arrived to visit him at the hospital, my eyes beheld a very sick man which did not coincide with what I had expected to find. As a minister, I had visited sick people in hospitals for some twenty-five years, but on that day when I saw David, my mind just couldn't justify with my feelings! I was determined though, not to allow my personal thoughts to win out over my faith. I searched for a word from God and then spoke it out to David. Looking back, I don't even remember exactly what I said to him, but David, being a strong man of God, held on to that word like a lifeline had been thrown to him. Whatever it was I said, it seemed to be the spark that ignited his resolve.

This fun and amazing book takes you on the remarkable journey of faith, perseverance and discovery of a man who defied the odds and achieved the success of the dreams which he thought had died with his youth. A man who literally fought his way back from the brink for himself, his family and those who mattered most to him. I hope his story, his wit and his wisdom on these pages will be as much an inspiration to you as it has been to me.

— Daryl Nicolet

Sr. Leader,
Faith Worship Center, Pepperell, MA

Preface

"I.C.U. to Marathon" is the magic bullet you've been waiting for! To solve all of your health issues, create domestic tranquility and get your whites whiter.

Maybe not.

This running book is not about running, it's not another fad diet, it's not a weight loss book, and it's not a fitness system or a pyramid scheme. I am not another guru with a new "clinically-proven scientific breakthrough" to seduce you with. Yours truly is not an expert, but if I had the chance, I would play one on TV. I hope you'll find my book inspiring, or at the very least, as entertaining as a cat might find a mouse stricken with arthritis to be, or a teenager with a "smartphone".

This is the story of a fat guy who became deathly ill in April of 2011, and nearly bought the farm. Despite some negative "expert" opinions from medical experts, that guy decided to make the most of his life, and eventually beat the odds.

That guy was — and is — me; however, I think in reading this book, you'll find that in many ways, it is a book about you, too.

The two years prior to writing "I.C.U. to Marathon" have been a unique part of life's journey. Educating myself about health, fitness and nutrition has been a process, through which, I have actually learned more about my faith in God, than why flavonoids are good for you. There has been a lot of *error and trial* as I focused on correcting unhealthy habits. Of course the road to running a marathon, even for a *healthy* person, is challenging; and for me, many would have argued, impossible.

Like so many others, I have often said, "If I had only known." We all seem to have twenty-twenty hindsight, do we not? This book represents a lot of time sifting through the myths, the mystery, the unbelievable claims, the science, and the practical day-to-day habits that make solid personal fitness possible. For instance, doctors say that each piece of bacon you eat takes a minute off your life. Based on that data, I should have died in 1886. Sometimes health is a matter of common sense, other times it is knowledge, and occasionally, it involves luck. Here is an example: One day I ate a large can of cashews and it cured my IBS symptoms.

From the day I left the Framingham Heart Center, I stubbornly desired to be healthy. On many of my treks around town, my route passes by the hospital where I had been in the I.C.U.. In my mind's eye I would see the monitors, tubes and wires. I would hear the beeping machines, the incessant echo of the intercom speakers in the hallways, and the condescending words of the doctors who tended to yet another pathetic fifty-something couch-potato that landed in their midst, and then as I pass by, I declare my health and wellbeing. My inner-voice crying out, "Never again!"

It's an honor to be selected to take a spot in the magazine rack in your bathroom. (If you are reading an eBook by the way, for $5.00 more you could have had a printed copy to leave on top of the tank and not have to balance your Nook on your hairy knees.) I hope you'll learn from my mistakes, enjoy reading about the convoluted road that got me into trouble in the first place, and the road that brought me back, nearly from the dead. I hope you find a laugh here and there — maybe even a laugh about yourself, if you're honest. But most importantly, I hope you find inspiration here; whether you choose to follow me to the starting line one day, or to just start making some smart, healthy choices in life. Sometimes it just helps to know that you're not the only one.

Introduction

I was a skinny kid growing up in Connecticut suburbia, just shy of five feet tall and weighing in at just 101 pounds in fourth grade. By the time high school graduation rolled around, I was six-feet, one-inch tall and weighed 165 pounds. I was a vigorously active growing boy, and I loved to eat! My short list included pizza, steak, swordfish, potatoes, most vegetables, hamburgers, hotdogs, salad, clam chowder and chocolate-just-about-anything! I drank Coke whenever it was available, and lots of milk. In fact, my parents kept a two-and-a-half gallon dispenser for milk on the top shelf of our coppertone side-by-side refrigerator to be sure there was always ample supply.

No one ever had to ring a dinner bell for me; I was always the first one hanging around the kitchen anxiously waiting for it to be served!

Breakfast when I was a kid (during the week), was typically a bowl of unsweetened cereal with milk, topped with a little sugar, along with a glass of orange juice, and on the weekend it was pancakes with maple syrup, or eggs and bacon. School lunches came from home with mom's signature white bread sandwiches, a piece of fruit, and milk in the Thermos of my *Flipper* lunch box.

Dinner at the Johndrow's was traditional American fare, usually consisting of one canned or frozen vegetable with rice or potatoes and some sort of meat. There were lots of tuna casseroles, meatloaves, frozen fish sticks, sloppy Joes, pastas and the ubiquitous staple of American suburbia, Hamburger Helper. Fresh fish was generally too expensive, but every so often we'd enjoy the occasional piece of swordfish which, to this day, I still maintain a passion for. In the summertime, I always looked forward to the coveted birch beer soda or pink lemonade, native-grown corn on the cob, mom's potato salad, and burgers or hot dogs off of our back yard charcoal grill. My folks had a little garden in the back yard too, where they grew tomatoes, cucumbers, summer squash, zucchini, green peppers and eggplant each season. Salad was always on the menu.

The coveted dessert was a treat for Saturday nights, which was usually ice cream, homemade apple pie or a tray of brownies.

During the holidays, my mom really worked hard in the kitchen making special dishes and treats. There was always a huge spread for Thanksgiving with a twenty-something pound turkey, gravy, stuffing, creamed onions (I know, who eats those?), mashed potatoes, peas, candied yams and tomato aspic! Christmas was even more elaborate with Stoli, and a variety of homemade cookies which mom exchanged with friends and neighbors. London broil was our traditional Christmas dinner with all the trimmings and homemade dinner rolls. New Year's Eve was another special occasion with chips and dip, shrimp cocktail, miniature hotdogs, cocktail breads, cheese spreads and enough alcohol to fill the Parisian sewer for a day.

To be fair, there were some foods I didn't like. I took a few years off from green peas after barfing them up on my plate at the Thanksgiving table back in '67. All I remember is that it was hard to tell them from the creamed onions after that. I am just glad they didn't come out my nose like the time when my classmate, Michael, got sick during lunch in fourth grade. I wish there was a video of that day — green peas and milk gushing from both his nostrils. That was worth a standing ovation! Twenty years later I gagged on my first piece of tofu; that's on the list now, too.

As a child I was very active. We rode bicycles around the neighborhood and often trekked the mile or so up to the center of town to buy candy (actually, rack cigars and *Playboy* magazines, truth be told), at the neighborhood drug store. Eventually, I would ride the six miles to high school and back. All the students in our town had recess until sixth grade and then gym twice a week starting in eighth grade. We played everything: dodge-ball, floor hockey, kickball, football, basketball, baseball, crab soccer and gymnastics. I confess, however, that I faked being sick, so I wouldn't have to square dance with cootie-infested girls (obviously, I got over that phobia in later years).

If it wasn't raining, there were football and baseball games with the neighbors in our backyard. In the winter months we'd play hockey on one of the local ponds, or go sledding, and on rare occasion, there was the Saturday ski trip to Powder Ridge, Catamount or Butternut Basin resorts. On summer family vacations, I could be found waterskiing on the lake from sun up to sun down. I played organized basketball in middle school, as well as being in a Saturday bowling league. When I was a little older, my parents let me buy a dirt bike, and I spent hours and hours racing around the sand pit across the street. My brother and I even mapped and cleared a motocross track, complete with jumps, hairpin turns, a water crossing and whoop-de-dos.

June 8, 1978

Out for a ride to cool off by catching a little air, and having a cigarette in my buddies' back yard.

Photo by: Fredrick Stone

Of course there were no video games in those days, and TV (the kind you had to get up from the couch and manually change the channels by actually turning a large knob with numbers on it that designated the dozen or so channels that were available, though we could only get in about half that many) was more of a Saturday morning distraction until nine o'clock, when we were allowed to go out to knock on the neighbor's front door. When we were kids, you just couldn't keep us indoors for long.

By the time I was eleven years old, I rode my motocross bike each day for a few hours after school. Rocketing the 220-pound beast at speeds of up to sixty-five miles per hour over twenty-foot jumps, firing across the mud flats, splashing through knee-high water, laying it out sideways on a berm or wrestling it though a series of whoop-de-dos on the back tire. It was one of my favorite sports.

When I wasn't on the motorcycle, I was at the rink — usually at four or five in the morning — for hockey practice. During high school I played on the varsity hockey team, and eventually played on my college team as well. My brother and I were a defense team to be reckoned with, and we loved the hard-hitting, fast action out there on the ice. Each summer we'd be off to hockey school for a few weeks where we played four to six hours every day. Despite a few stitches, some broken teeth, a couple of sprains, and a cracked rib, hockey is still my favorite game to play.

I've had a number of jobs over the years. I taught high school music for three years at a private school, worked part-time as a disc jockey at a local radio station, and even did a stint as a photographer. As a young adult though, my main occupation was carpentry. For a starving artist, it was always a good plan to have a well-paying trade to fall back on.

So what happened?

One day I was sitting at the dinner table, minding my own business, and my metabolism crashed and burned. After that, I went from 170 pounds to about 220 in a year's time. It was the perfect storm: midlife, transferring from the activity of carpentry to a sedentary desk job, and quitting smoking all at the same time, and my metabolic ship struck the iceberg and sank into a non-alcoholic beer belly (sometimes, late at night when it was really quiet, I could hear little voices calling out "Man the life boats! Women and children first!"). I struggled with my weight and health from that point on. My blood pressure shot up, my cholesterol too, and I felt bloated, fat, and tired. Exercise? My passion for vigorous

Photo by: Sarah J. Thornington-Cericola

September 7, 1994

Steve Jobs was my hero, and I loved my Mac! This was my first day at a desk job. I was a carpenter just the day before, and suddenly, I was a computer nerd. I had just gotten back from the lawyer's office after having incorporated my new company, Virtual Cape Cod.

(and at times, arguably, dangerous) diversions had deteriorated into a complete revulsion of anything that caused me to break a sweat.

In 2000 I was able to get my weight back down to 190 through dieting alone. Strict portion control and generally just eating less of what always had been, and the weight dropped off quickly. I starved myself in the mornings by skipping breakfast and existed on unsweetened coffee until lunch — which consisted of a twelve-ounce can of sparkling water and a granola bar. Picture me eating a Happy Meal instead of a Supersized Quarter Pounder Meal from McDonald's for dinner. The upside was the toys that I accumulated and gave to my children (well, most of them, anyway), which made us all very happy.

April 12, 2008

A nice day for a walk and some fresh air, the girls and I went to the waterfalls on the Charles River in South Natick. I look terrible.

Photo by: Zoe Johndrow

By the stroke of midnight on New Year's Eve 2004, I had ballooned back up to more than 230 pounds. At that time, my wife and I were fans of the Dr. Phil Show. We started using *The Ultimate Weight Loss Solution* which is primarily portion control and low-calorie meals combined with working out at the gym for thirty minutes, three times a week. We stopped eating rice, potatoes and white bread, and increased our fruit and vegetables consumption. We bought low-calorie and low-fat everything — except, of course, coffee!

My best efforts eventually rolled the scale back down to 199 pounds. I was looking better, feeling pretty good and I purchased all these great skinny clothes to replace all of the then-all-too-baggy stuff that just hung off of me. Learning a bit about food, I was not starving like I was before. Then, I had my first overuse injury: *plantar fasciitis*, a foot disorder causing pain in the heel. It hurt to get out of bed, it hurt to walk, and it hurt to run. The doctor said it was probably from using the treadmill at high inclines and not stretching.

For the next five or six years I gave up exercising altogether after trying a number of treatments for the planter fasciitis, including stretching, a night splint, shoe inserts, cortisone injections, ultrasound, massage and various other therapies; nothing seemed to work. My increasing weight made the pain even worse which inspired me to become even more of a sloth. Slowly, I slipped back into most of my old eating habits. I started drinking soda, eating out without giving my food choices any thought, and increasing my junk food intake. I was having an illicit affair with a freckle-faced siren named Little Debbie, and forgetting food portion sizes altogether. In my mind, I was convinced that I would one day get a handle on my weight. I just didn't feel like putting in the required effort.

Fast-forward a little, and that's where this story begins.

CHAPTER ONE

This is Me at the Aquarium

There I sat in front of my computer, looking at a picture on Facebook in which my eldest daughter had tagged me - all 276 pounds of me. My two chins and forty-two inches of girth were not very becoming. In the photo, too, was my then-six-year-old, Charlotte. She was just a kid who loved her dad. I felt bad that she had never really known me fit and trim. My friends and family were kind enough not to post comments like "Oh look, I didn't know they had a whale at the New England Aquarium!"

It had been years since I really looked at myself in a mirror. Probably, to be more accurate, I looked, but really didn't pay any attention (denial can be a powerful filter). People had long-since stopped saying things like, "Lookin' good, David!" I made excuses for my appearance, most of them were pretty lame. In fact, I stopped caring about it all together. Many years before, I had laughed as I thought of Mike Warnke saying, "You can always tell when a guy is on the level, his bubble is in the middle." As I sat there contemplating asking my daughter to remove the photo, I didn't think fat was the least bit funny anymore.

The feeling of being old was nagging at me too; the fatigue, the depression, and the fear of chronic sickness were constant quiet-time companions. I was on a slow train heading toward my eventual death, and I didn't know where the tracks would lead along the way to my inevitable destination.

Oh sure, I had sincere talks with my doctor about my blood pressure and various other test results that showed I wasn't as healthy as I hoped I was. With the sphygmomanometer registering 145/100 the doc wrote a script for Lisinopril 2.5 mg. "You need to knock off twenty pounds and get this blood pressure down," he scolded me. "You are technically obese and in danger of developing heart disease or having a stroke."

March 23, 2009

Today I went with the girls to the New England Aquarium. Look how awful the wide-angle lens made me look!

I walked back to the car thinking about how good I looked in 1990. In my mind's eye, I still looked that way. I thought about how, back in high school, I used to play hockey for hours at a time. In the year 2009, I didn't like to do much of anything physical. I watched television with my youngest, but we didn't get any real exercise. In a short-lived heroic effort to lose some weight (much of which would be the removal of my doctor from my back), I starved myself for a few days and skipped desserts for a while, I even ate an apple one day and thought, "this isn't working", I had been dieting all morning!

My weight had caused other problems, too. I felt tired all the time, I was lethargic, my joints ached, and my back would go out badly enough to end me up in bed for the better part of a week. The orthopedic surgeon recommended spinal fusion if my condition persisted. I had gained so much weight that I couldn't tie my own shoes, nor did I fit comfortably in the front seat of my Honda Civic.

One cold winter, some of the families from church planned to get together on the frozen lake for ice skating, a friendly game of hockey, and some roasted hotdogs on the fire. I hadn't skated in years; I didn't even own any skates anymore. Purchasing a used pair and a hockey stick, I showed up lakeside for the event remembering my glory days and looking forward to gliding gracefully across the ice and mixing it up again on the lake. I sat down on a wooden bench and started lacing up my skates. I was so fat that, as I leaned over, I crushed my diaphragm, making it hard to breathe. I felt like a turtle on his back, gasping for air. I finally finished the last knot, caught my breath, and skated out to join the game.

We took the Green Line.

Photo by: David Johndrow

It wasn't but a few minutes later that, when I made a sharp left turn to maneuver the puck past an opponent, the blade of my left skate snapped right off, shattering the post and sending me hard on to the ice like so much road kill. I was so embarrassed; I didn't even stay for the cookout.

The aches and pains were growing more frequent. It seemed every x-ray showed signs of arthritis: my back, my knee, my shoulder and even the temporomandibular joint in my jaw. I honestly could not remember the last time I felt good, save sucking down a Coffee Coolada with whipped cream on a summer Sunday drive. Looking back now, I never really realized just how badly I felt - it seemed normal - I slowly adapted, just like the proverbial frog in the pot of boiling water (besides, I was resolved to my advancing years; it all comes with the territory, so to speak. Right?). But all in all, the most notable effect of my unfit lifestyle was that I lost most of my self esteem.

Here's Your Sign

I was obese. I could no longer deny it, it was the 600-pound gorilla in the room, and I had to acknowledge it. But coming to terms with that fact was not a lot of fun. My little one said to me one day as we are sitting watching television, "I love your fat, daddy!" My wife started to interject, our eyes met, but whatever correction we could come up with just didn't seem to fit the situation, so I just squeezed my daughter and gave her a kiss.

One day I decided to work up a test much like those that alcoholics take in self-help groups, and then take it myself. As you might guess, I failed. The test went something like this:

1. Does your navel make an echo? *Yes.*

2. Can you purchase flattering clothing at Victoria's Secret or Men's Warehouse? Can you even find any?
No, not without ending up on Funny or Die.

3. Do you have your own postal code? *Not yet.*

4. Does your talking bathroom scale yell, "Holy Crap!" when you step on it? *I don't have a talking scale.*

5. Have you been selected for the new Jenny Craig commercial? *No.*

6. Do you buy Devil Dogs or Ho Ho's in bulk?
Just once at the wholesale club.

7. Can you be seen from the International Space Station?
I don't want to know.

8. Do you think that Little Debbie's Nutter Butters are protein bars? *They're not?*

9. Does your shadow weigh as much as a sack of potatoes?
I couldn't get it on the scale at the truck stop.

10. When you go to the zoo, do the elephants wolf-whistle and throw you peanuts?
No, but I think the rhino was eyeing me.

11. If you are lying on the beach, do Greenpeace volunteers keep pouring water on you and trying to push you back into the ocean? *I wore a Led Zeppelin t-shirt just in case.*

12. Do your stretch marks have stretch marks? *Yes.*

If you laughed at any of these questions, you might be overweight.

In 2000 I went to buy new pants for work, having outgrown two more pairs. I settled on some with forty-two inch stretch waist bands. For a guy who had once fit into thirty-one inches, it was demoralizing. Looking at myself in the dressing room mirror caused a flood of bad feelings, "nothing will ever look good on me", I said to myself. Without even trying on the second pair, I grabbed them and headed for the cash register to avoid further torturing myself. Passing through the underwear aisle, the self-talk continued. The size tags on the pants were haunting me all the way to the checkout line.

The consequences of my bad lifestyle choices were adding up, so I decided to try a high-protein diet of my own fabrication, something that I'd feel comfortable with. I ate lots of bacon, eggs and cheese along with everything else that I was already routinely eating. Needless to say, it didn't work. But, really I wanted to change, to look in the mirror and look slim and trim and, yeah, even feel a little bit sexy like the good ol' days, but I would grab a fistful of belly fat (which felt like a shrink-wrapped pork loin at the grocery store), and just shake my head lamenting, "I will never be thin again."

November 20, 2010

We had a late birthday celebration for my youngest daughter that day. I tried not to eat the cake and ice cream, but I just couldn't help myself.

Photo by: Zoe Johndrow

Changing your lifestyle, no matter how important you know it is to do, and no matter how determined you might be, is really, really hard to do. In 1980 I quit drinking a day at a time, and in 1994 I quit smoking cigarettes. Emotionally, it often seems impossible to make a permanent lifestyle change, and my addictive personality makes it even more difficult.

I've discovered, however, that there are many approaches to making successful life changes. Whether it is a support group, reward-based shaping, gastric bypass, using a life coach, a photo of

January 22, 2011

My daughter, Zöe, came over to have dinner with us after work. I told her an off-color joke.

a bathing beauty on the 'fridge, or a combination of methods, it all starts with the hard decision to just do it. There are times when talking with those who have already successfully done it makes it easier, but sometimes it can make it even harder, too - I don't need anyone talking about food; especially when I'm not thinking about it at that moment!

The problem with eating is that you can't just quit. It's impossible to put eating behind you like so many other bad habits. Everyone eats because everyone has to eat! If we don't eat, we die. Unlike smoking, it's socially acceptable to eat in every corner of the world, even in restaurants. To make things worse, the government has so far not banned food commercials on TV, or vending machines that spew Little Debbies and candy bars, and you don't have to show I.D. to buy Twinkees. Eating is part of everyday life no matter who you are. With so many delicious choices, I felt trapped.

When you don't know anything about nutrition, it's easy to become a target for misinformation, and there's plenty of it out there. Add a layer of excuses, a teaspoon of procrastination and a little denial (okay, maybe a *lot* of denial), and it's simple to see how I, and millions of others, ended up as potential stand-ins for *Free Willy*.

Big food marketing campaigns target us with shiny packaging using terms like "low fat", "low-caloric", "low sodium", "healthy", "organic", and "all natural", which are subliminally appealing (and often grossly stretching the truth). Those messages played on me with every bite, influencing my food decisions. I thought I knew what was healthy, didn't I? The list typed itself out in my mind's eye: salad, fruit, granola, yogurt, milk, cheese and eggs. I thought I knew how to lose weight: go on a starvation diet loaded with protein! And never to be on the list were fast food, soda or any kind or dessert, right? It seemed like it was time to suck it up, and get with the program.

I realized that I didn't actually know anyone that was really healthy. My mother had become a heart-healthy eater after my stepfather had bypass surgery in the early '90s. They ate salad, fruit and fish, and stopped going to Arby's. My sister was a vegetarian, though we only ate together a few times. Once she came to stay with us and tried to kill me with chunks of tofu. Most folks I knew got sick from time to time, and a lot of them were overweight. Of course someone was always going on a diet. I was confused. And worse, I felt helpless in fighting the fitness battle - let alone win it.

On the medical front, my blood work wasn't looking too good either. Though it was within safe ranges, my blood sugar, my cholesterol and my vitamin levels were all border line. My blood pressure had always been on the verge of hypertension which doctors had been warning me about for years.

It was easier to have a hernia exam than to talk with the doctor about what I needed to do. Truthfully, my doctor didn't look to be in the best of shape either (which didn't bode well for his credibility in my mind). I just kept hoping there would be no bad news. "If I could just stay where I was at," I thought, "I'll be okay." Every year the blood test numbers inched closer to the line, closer to the need for medication, and another step closer to the increased medical risks such as diabetes, stroke and heart disease – even my cancer risk was increasing. It scared me.

Other than brushing my teeth each day, I hadn't done anything one would consider to be exercise for years. Except for a few miles on my honeymoon in 2003, I hadn't taken a hike or ridden a bicycle since 1999. I walked when I had to, but I sat every chance I got. I always took the closest parking space to the door. I still do that even when I go to the gym to use the treadmill. How screwed up is that? In an emergency, I might have been able to run a few hundred yards. Certainly not the 10.6-second 100-yard dash I could do in high school. Sure, I had my kill-yourself-in-the-gym-diet in 2004, but since my foot injury, there has been nothing which could be called exercise. I couldn't even keep up with my wife on a walk with a tiny six-pound Chihuahua. We lived on the third floor, and going up and down once or twice a day was plenty for this guy. We used to get the grocery store to deliver just so we didn't have to carry twenty bags up the stairs! When my kids asked me why I didn't do anything, I told them I was a recovering workaholic. Yeah, pretty pathetic, I know.

CHAPTER TWO

Sweat is Your Fat Crying

In February of 2011, my doctor gave me another stern warning about my weight and bad report regarding my hypertension. He added Hydrochlorothiazide to the Lisinopril I was already taking. A hopeless feeling swept over me - poor me, I was awash in a sea of unfairness. Weighing in 111 pounds heavier than I was when I graduated high school, I was disgusted with myself. In the privacy of the exam room, I looked in the mirror as I got dressed. What I saw was more humiliating than the rectal and hernia exams I had just had. It was time to make a few drastic changes in the way I ate. The doctor insisted I lose weight, but he didn't say how. I thought back to my previous attempts which were successful, but not long lasting, which begs the question: just how successful were they... really?

About that same time, my wife was attending a 5:00 AM gym class and was losing weight - and looking ~~hot~~ really good! One evening, during our after dinner tea, we decided to attend a circuit cardio class together, twice a week at the YMCA. It was after work, so they had babysitting available for our little one while we worked out.

The shrink-wrapped pork loin had to go! That was my motto (it's good to have mottos, I'm told). A few days before the class began, a bunch of slender (read: skinny-assed) trainers gave us a chalk-talk on nutrition. Divide your plate into thirds with two servings of vegetables and one of protein, watch your portion sizes and skip the fast food. I already knew that stuff, it was not very helpful. Well, not about the plate. McDonald's doesn't have plates. I preferred to envision the content of pizza boxes and whatever plasticware that take-out came in.

The first day of class arrived, and I had been gone all day for work. Commuting to and from Boston for hours and spending nine hours in a desk chair, there was no time for dinner before I had to be at the "Y" for class.

I bent, twisted, gyrated, jumped up and down, perspired for an hour and finally got my sneakers tied. Me in my synthetic Wal-Mart training suit and cheap white sneakers, I opened the door for my wife and daughter. We headed over to my very first "In It to Lose It" class. We warmed up on the treadmill first, and I clocked three tenths of a mile in fifteen minutes. Yeah, baby, feel the burn! And then the class actually began.

> I used to say, "today is one of those days I feel like having a 6-pack", and then I'd head to the gym to make one.

It was tough! I was huffing and puffing like I was dying after five jumping jacks - not a good start. Two minutes into it, and I nearly blew my cookies. I was too fat to touch my toes. The soccer moms in the class in their leotards and leg warmers turned their noses up at me. My body was crying out, "Leave me alone!" Over the years, my fat and I had become good friends, and rather attached to one another. This was a going to be a painful break up.

Had I known what was coming, I would have left my water bottle closer to the floor, and also brought an oxygen tank. I felt a little comforted when I noticed that they kept a defibrillator only inches away. In my mind, over my wife's sobbing, I could hear the EMT's shouting "clear!", as my lifeless body bounced off the floor.

After thus far controlling the urge to vomit, I had a few other random thoughts. For instance, the one-to-ten "pain scale" used in hospitals needs to be extended to fifteen! Webster, the writer of the definition for the word "agony", was certainly well under fifty-years-old when he came up with it, and had never subjected himself to the abuse of such a class at his local "Y" (assuming there were any in his day). Today's editors need to add a fourth definition: "just freakin' shoot me!"

I got home that evening and didn't feel like eating - sort of like a New Year's morning hangover.

In the morning, the sun glistened on the dew-covered grass. I'm sure it was lovely, but I didn't care, everything hurt - even things that I didn't recall having had in places that I didn't remember them being in. They all hurt.

In addition to sessions with "Attila the freakin' Hun", I added two more workouts each week, remembering my motto about the shrink-wrapped pork loin. I was doing pushups, squats, lunges, jumping jacks and crunches (where you try and head-butt your own crotch), as well as walking and running on the treadmill. It took several weeks, but new sounds came from my body in the form of words and primal sentences without actually swallowing my tongue. As an evolving sports linguist, "this sucks" was my first complete sentence. I intend to contact Sir Hugh Beaver to request a record review for the use of this uniquely expressive phrase, in which my usage certainly must have eclipsed anything listed in the Guinness Book of World Records for the frequency of its utterance within in a single hour.

Workouts kept on sucking. On the positive side, though, I had lost forty-five pounds! My top running speed on the treadmill was up to seven miles per hour from zero. I went from less than a mile per workout to around three in forty-five minutes. And the most notable change, everything that hurt before, hurt more than before. I sat at the dinner table with my chicken breast and salad, and I remember feeling a little invigorated — a little more alive.

Then there was the food, glorious food which had to be dealt with. God in his infinite wisdom had my local McDonald's razed about same time I started working out. My favorite drive-thru restaurant, the one just a few miles from my home, was gone! My wife and I figured out how to order kid's meals from our favorite chain restaurants. We would just have the little one call — three meals, under $11! We worked at smaller portions and better quality food; it was paying off.

Once you've begun cutting calories and eating smaller portions, how will you know that you've entered the Diet Zone? Here's another self test to help (you'll thank me later).

1. Does the dog food look appetizing?

2. Do you try to eat the crumbs from the bottom of every package and lick the bottom of the yogurt cup (crushing it down if your tongue doesn't reach that far)?

3. Have you extended the 5-Second Rule to 40 minutes?

4. Do you only weigh yourself after going "number two"?

5. Have you purposely tripped a skinny person on the escalator at the mall?

6. Have you blocked restaurant commercials on your cable remote?

7. Do you "suck it in" and look at yourself sideways in the mirror?

8. Have you dreamt of a vacation to the Food Court at Disney World?

9. Have you thought of eating foods sacrificed to pagan idols?

10. Have you started to read the Bible to see what foods will be on the table at the Great Banquet in the clouds?

If you answered "YES" to two or more of these questions, you might have a clue as to what I was going through those first couple of weeks. The change takes time, but it's worth it.

I still had a lot of bad information about health, fitness and a proper diet. I thought I knew what foods were good for me, and which ones were bad. I was further convinced that the lack of exercise was in large part the cause of my obesity. I was wrong about pretty much everything that I thought I knew to be healthy.

Despite my fitness IQ (ignorance quotient), I continued to make slow, but steady progress. I ate the wrong things, I didn't do very many exercises correctly, and I certainly didn't know anything about warm ups or stretching. I fell back on the little information I had gleaned from the doctor, the trainer and that twenty minute seminar on portion sizes from the YMCA nutritionist – and my fifth grade health class. In the back of my mind, I was still looking for the magic pill, and the easy way out to weight loss. I believed that losing weight would make me healthy. I was only partially correct.

What I eventually found was that what I *ate* was 80%, or more likely 90%, of the weight loss equation. I was focused on exercise, but what I really needed to learn about was food. The truth seemed to be this: If I exercise for a few hours a week, that is only 10% or 20% of my weekly caloric equation. However, if I ate correctly, that was 80% or 90% of the metabolic puzzle. The math seemed simple. A guy my size could burn 2,000 calories doing nothing for a day. I could ingest 2,000 calories eating a meal with bread, salad and dessert at any of the chain restaurants. I could do it eating half a large pizza! If I ran for two solid hours (13.1 miles, a half-marathon), I could earn that pizza. It seemed logical to me that food was a great place to focus most of my energy. The small rudder of the big ship was finally starting to turn.

My wife and I spent the next few months working out while eating the diet that we knew how to. Despite our ignorance, there was enough progress to keep us going. I honestly don't believe that most overweight or obese people think about getting healthy or fit until they've had a health scare. I do believe that they think about getting thinner and sexier, though. There are many motivations for losing weight. Looks, clothes, a special event such as a wedding, to become more attractive in your own eyes - or someone else's - but few decide to get fit as their primary objective.

When I decided to make a change, I spent some time thinking about what I really looked like. Occasionally I would stumble across some change in my body that excited me, like collarbones for instance (I always knew they were under there somewhere, I remembered them from long ago). Despite the victories on the scale, waist size was *the* benchmark for my personal success. Eventually I thought, I want to tuck in my shirt without feeling like a blob. There were some body parts that I was anxious to leave behind. If you haven't lived in the ethereal world of the obese and overweight, we have our own non-medical vocabulary. To help you better understand and communicate in this ever-expanding realm, I've pieced together a quick reference for you, much like the "French Survival Phrases" sort of handbooks for world travelers.

Glossary of Body Parts
You Can Live Without!

Being overweight like I was is unhealthy and dangerous. I suppose one might have a surgical procedure, in which a body part is removed. However; by eating right and getting regular exercise, you can give yourself some free and painless cosmetic surgery.

You might have heard of some these anatomical abnormalities.

Beer Shelf Butt: A Kardashian butt that sticks out far enough to hold a sixteen-ounce can of Miller Light.

Spare Tire: The obvious protruding belly. The problem is that for some of us, it's a spare tire for a Boeing 747 jetliner.

Dickeydoo: When your belly sticks out further than your dickey do.

Dunlap Disease: When your belly has "done lapped" over your belt.

Thunder Thighs: At first I thought it was a Biblical creature, but it turns out to be the opposite of "chicken legs".

Love Handles: This is the fat around the kidney area which keeps us from escaping a hormone-fueled mate or raging attack dog.

Prayer Shelf: A belly large enough to fold your hands and rest them on comfortably when you sit.

Double Bubbles: Men or women with two boob bumps from wearing a bra that is 2 sizes too small.

Groin Blobs: Genital covering to protect us from 3-foot-two-inch children.

Arm Danglers: Sometimes known as the "reverse biceps". In the south they're known as, "bingo wings".

Expansion Tank: These are fat blobs that seem to show up in unusual places - if you have them, you know what I am talking about.

Ring Roll: The little rolls that keep your rings so secure they can't be removed. The up side is, you can't lose them in the garbage disposal (your rings, that is).

Intake Port: Your mouth. When you change your relationship with food, it becomes a way to savor good food and enjoy it.

Trailer Brakes: The fat on your backside that hangs over the chair edge so you don't slide out.

Man Boobs (or Moobs): Boobs on a man.

Chin Coaster: 2 or more chins.

Cankles: Calves and ankles combined.

Pants Pockets: They look like pockets when you are not wearing pants. If they get stretch marks, they are known as zippered pockets.

Cup Holder: A navel vortex. Mine could have easily held a double shot glass.

Talons: Unclipped toenails because you haven't seen them for a few years, and can't reach them anyway.

Tharms: Arms as big as thunder thighs.

Fat Fingers: Used for inadvertently typing two or three keys at a time.

Muffin Tops: A cascading blend of belly and hip fat created by tight-waisted pants or belts.

Junk in the Trunk: Just means it's a bad idea to wear a thong.

BOBIF: Big ol' butt in front. Sometimes known as a "frass" or "front bum".

Blegs: A bum and legs combined.

Wobbly Bits (UK): Anything that is still moving once you have stopped.

CHAPTER THREE

They Weren't Kidding

It was early Saturday afternoon at the local YMCA, as I worked my way past the 2.0 mile mark on the treadmill. My stomach was feeling a little sour, but I pressed on for the remainder of the hour. Workout completed: 3.37 miles (5K) in forty-four minutes. Not a bad time for a fifty-two-year-old guy weighing 245 pounds. I had been working out for a few months by that time, and had lost thirty-one pounds. Despite feeling a little nauseous, the burn felt great as I fantasized about the good news Mr. Scale was going to give me at my next weigh-in.

After a shower, it was off to meet my daughter for a birthday dinner ninety miles away. We went to her favorite restaurant. I skipped the solid food and ordered some soup and iced tea as I wasn't feeling very good at all. I pulled into the driveway at home at 6:00 PM and went straight to bed, but awoke sick to my stomach at about 11:00 that evening, so I rolled out of bed and made my way to the bathroom. "It's just a 24-hour bug," I thought, "some of the folks at work and at church have had it. I'll be fine." There were about a dozen trips on the ivory bus (ours is a stick shift). As I lay spent on the bathroom floor I thought again, "a little sleep and some ginger ale, and I will be over this."

Sunday was a blur, although I did feel a little better in the morning. I continued to drink ginger ale and water, as I lay in bed.

I even went downstairs to try a little chicken broth at the dinner table. By the time evening rolled around though, I was back in the bathroom feeling extremely nauseous. I took my blood pressure medication and went back to bed. I don't really remember what happened during the night, but I remember waking up on Monday morning just as the sun was coming up. I made a feeble call to work, to let them know I wasn't coming in; it was 6:00 AM. I spent the morning lying on my back feeling miserable. Because I had been throwing up, my chest was burning. I put a glass of ice water on it, which helped the pain subside a little.

At 9:00 AM, I was able to get my doctor's office on the phone to ask what they thought I should do. "Come in at 3:00 this afternoon, or go to the emergency room," the receptionist said. I phoned my wife to take me to the E.R. I arrived there at about 11:00 AM. They thought I had the flu, and gave me a germ mask. In the waiting room I fell off the bench. That's when they took me right in and went over my symptoms with me. "Tired, dizzy, vomiting, and chest pain, more pain here, here, here and here. Other than that, I feel great!" I told the nurse.

"Okay," said the nurse, after she introduced two student nurses. I guess she was trying to discourage them from entering the nursing field by having a half-naked-smelly-fat-man take off his t-shirt. They gave me an I.V. and shot some Kytril in there to calm my stomach. Man, I wish I had that when I was drinking! Next they took my vital signs - blood pressure, pulse, etc. - and hooked me up to an E.K.G.

"Ladies," the R.N. said to the student nurses, "I need you to leave the room." She then turned to my wife and said, "Ma'am, I would like you to have a seat here", pointing to the chair at the foot of the bed. "Sir, everything is going to be alright, but you are having congestive heart failure."

I didn't hear her say that.

Did I?

A wave of uncertainty rolled over me, as I tried to decide if I was really in trouble. The R.N. shoved my mouth full of aspirin and Plavix, and slipped some nitro under my tongue. Then she hooked me up to oxygen.

There was a lot of incomprehensible medical talk as two doctors came in to look at me. My blood pressure was at one-hundred over fifty-eight, and my blood oxygen was severely low...my thoughts trailed off momentarily. I looked over at my wife. She was just quiet as she sat there shouldering the weight of the unknown.

Yeah, I was really in trouble - big trouble.

"The Paramedics Will Be Here In a Few Minutes to Transport You to the Heart Trauma Center."

The sirens wailed as the paramedic talked to me about my family. We raced across the city. My wife followed somewhere behind in the family car. I can't imagine what was going through her mind in those moments. They slid me onto the operating table and began the catheterization surgery. The cardiologist said, yeah we'll get you "stented up", and probably have to take you to Beth Israel Hospital for a quadruple bypass..."

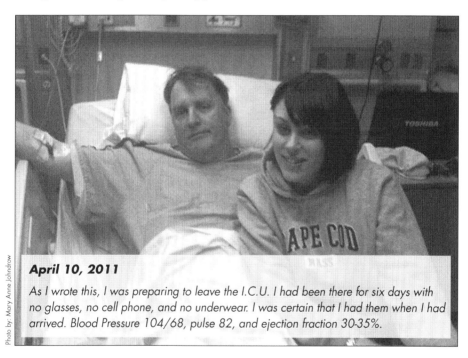

April 10, 2011

As I wrote this, I was preparing to leave the I.C.U. I had been there for six days with no glasses, no cell phone, and no underwear. I was certain that I had them when I had arrived. Blood Pressure 104/68, pulse 82, and ejection fraction 30-35%.

Photo by: Mary Anne Johndrow

There was the flickering of a TV monitor just above my head. I had enough drugs where I was a little in-and-out as all of this transpired. I tried not to think about the sharp surgical instruments so close to the family jewels. I imagined the orange tape as a landing strip for some devastatingly huge medical contraption. I had a flash of them painting something on my legs. I secretly feared that when I woke up, that it would look like skinny jeans on Rod Stewart.

"Well that is amazing, David. You have the arteries of a 17-year-old." I opened my eyes to see my wife standing there as the cardiologist gave the prognosis.

"Well, I would like to take them (my arteries) to Kentucky Fried Chicken, and get them into their twenties", I replied. "I take them everywhere I go."

I Do Love Fentanyl!

"You have what is known as a Myocarditis, and one chamber of your heart is virtually paralyzed. We are going to put you into the intensive care unit for a few days to see if the virus subsides."

Twenty-four hours later I sat in bed talking to the cardiologist. I was on twelve liters of oxygen per hour and hadn't been able to eat anything since the soup I had with my daughter three days earlier (which I'd probably thrown up later that evening, anyway).

"David, given the fact that you have one of the largest heart muscles I have ever seen, and the fact that, except for the infection, everything else is very healthy, you are lucky." (Read: exercise saved your life.) He went on to say that my ejection fraction was about 20% to 30%, and normal is around 60% to 70%. I really don't remember the rest of what he said. What I do remember is that the words "lucky to be alive" just kept ringing in my ears.

On Tuesday, April fifth, my friend and pastor, Daryl Nicolet, drove down to visit me. There I lay with my nasal cannula delivering life-giving oxygen; various monitoring devices stuck everywhere, and the flurry of busy nurses and doctors all about.

We had a nice chat about where I was in all this. He prayed for me just before he left. As he prayed I could feel the anointing of God, and I had a picture (internal vision) in my spirit: It was my heart, and swirling around it were my heart enzymes. In that still small voice I heard the Lord say, "You will completely recover." I shared it with Daryl and he agreed. "I am not worried," he said. He left me to be with my own thoughts.

As the nurses came to check on me, review my symptoms and check my surgical wound for bleeding, I watched a little television and messed with my laptop which my wife had brought in for me. I was feeling a little better. I had another E.K.G., an x-ray and an echocardiogram (ultrasound). The doctor came to visit the next morning and asked me, "How are you feeling?"

"A little better. I am hoping for a pair of clean underwear to-day too."

He smiled. "Well it looks like you made some tremendous progress since you got here. Your ejection fraction is up from the twenties to the thirties."

"When can I leave?"

"We'd like to see it in the forties."

I was in the I.C.U. for six nights, and then they let me go home. When I arrived at the house, I went upstairs to my bedroom and took off my dirty-feeling clothes. I pulled off some of the dozens of E.K.G. contacts - they were everywhere. I finally headed for the shower. As I stood there, I just cried. I don't know exactly why. I was relieved to be home. I guess I'd missed the simple things. Maybe the gravity of what really happened had suddenly hit me. I took a long and glorious shower and cried some more. On the way out I got on the scale, 244 pounds. "That sucks!" Especially considering that I hadn't really eaten for a week!

April 24, 2011

Easter Sunday. We had a nice buffet din-ner, but I was so tired, I just needed to go home and take a long nap. On a strict diet that didn't include coffee – I was seriously jonesing for a caffeine fix.

That night I slept in the relative quiet compared to all the noise I had experienced at the hospital - the bed checks, automatic vitals, evening medication and constant announcements blaring over the public address speakers.

It felt nice to be at home. I slept a lot. I took another nap, and when I woke up on Sunday morning, I dreamt I was drowning. My chest hurt and I was very anxious. I asked my wife to get me to the E.R. Another E.K.G. in triage, and while that was being done, my little girl got a nosebleed. I asked the nurse if we could get a two-for-one deal, as she found her a cot to lie down on. It was a Johndrow circus!

The medical staff took another x-ray, another E.K.G., and another blood test. Six or seven hours later I was home again. My lungs had just filled up with fluid and that is what was causing me chest pain. My heart, however, was doing about the same as when I was released.

I was on a half dozen medications including diuretics, beta-blockers, A.C.E. inhibitors and blood thinners. Although I wanted to believe it was all going to turn out alright, it just didn't look good. I would lie in my room and wonder if I would ever recover. I didn't even have the energy to care. I was depressed, as my life seemed to be spinning out of control. Of course I did what I could to manage the things I was able to, the rest was done by my wife, or it didn't get done at all.

Boston Marathon 2011 - A Reason to Run

For the first time, I went to watch some of the 27,000 runners in the annual Boston Marathon. I had lived within a mile of the route for five years. Held on Patriots' Day, an obscure Massachusetts holiday on which I usually had to work, so I'd always missed all the excitement. In the days leading up to this massive event, I watched as town workers, road crews and vendors were setting up porta-potties, stockpiling police barriers, and placing skids of bottled water out along Route 135 as I drove into the city each day to work.

On race morning there were police cars at every crossroad ready to close the intersections to traffic as the runners approached. Making one's way into the city, there were dozens of buses filled with runners heading out to the official starting line in Hopkinton, 26.2 miles from the finish line at Copley Square in downtown Boston.

My oldest daughter dropped me off a couple of blocks from the barricades. There, a local bank was handing out cowbells and balloons (thank God there were no vuvuzelas like the World Cup!

Clearly Beantown was not ready for that). I waited in line for a complimentary cowbell, and then walked down to the "T" station for a view of something I had never seen or even imagined. A State Police cruiser led the elite runners, the winner having averaged just less than thirteen miles per hour, setting a record of two hours, three minutes and two seconds!

Amongst the front runners was American Ryan Hall. He finished fourth, just about a minute behind the leader. I had read about his personal faith and his running injuries, but here I was watching him in action. It moved me.

The marathon was not just runners in a race, but a fascinating drama which was unfolding. Think of a stadium emptying out onto a two-lane state highway in which everyone is running at about ten miles per hour. There are cowbells clanging and endless waves of applause as droves of athletes made their way past the 10-kilometer marker. Amidst the sea of excitement were families with inspirational posters, friends and loved ones hoping to get a high-five in with runners of every age and ability. Strangers shouting encouragement as they connected with something the runner was wearing. "Go team Rett!", "Great pace, David!" An endless array of colors, an ocean of sweating faces and adrenaline-fueled excitement - that was the 2011 Boston Marathon!

I was tracking two friends, both in their fifties, as they trekked even closer to Copley Square. It was hard to find them in the seemingly endless river of tank tops. They both finished with personal best times, though hours after the elite runners.

There was something emotional about it all. Being up close, standing on the sidewalk, you could read tattoos and sportswear brand names. Being front row to the visible intensity of personal strength and straining emotion was energizing, as we watched the sweat drip from their foreheads. Looks of determination, joy and passion flowed from some, while others seemed to be in their own worlds, apart from all that was going on around them.

Except for the elites, it seemed to me, that most everyone was running for a reason that was far deeper than winning, or best times; there was something greater.

Suddenly there was a loud applause and our focus was on those in wheelchairs. In particular, one was being pushed by a runner!

It was Dick and Rick Hoyt. Rick has cerebral palsy and his father pushes him along the race route. The dynamic duo has competed in marathons and triathlons together for decades. There is a memorial statue of the pair at Boston's Logan Airport.

To the delight of the crowd, there are all sorts of costumes, one runner sported a white robe and sandals — God only knows. Soon after, there was a man, a tall man, a *very* tall man in pink tights and a tutu. I can only imagine that he was running for breast cancer awareness (at least I hoped that he was).

There were survivors of cancer, heart disease, and those running in remembrance of loved ones passed on. The dedication to helping and remembering others was inspiring.

A man ran with a large American flag which could only slow him down. Another was a firefighter running in full gear including a Scott air-pack, coat, boots and a helmet. There was a U.S. Marine unit that ran in full combat gear, and packs in memory of a comrade lost in Iraq.

For the sake of love, many felt that the pain of a marathon run was one way to get in touch the pain of those that had suffered in this world.

I am not a big fan of Christian apparel, however; I saw a t-shirt that said "I Run Because He Gave His Life For Me", and on the back "26.2 Miles of Prayer, Stop Me And Ask". I thought to myself, who would give up precious minutes on a time clock for the sake of another?

I walked the mile back home with my wife and daughter. My youngest pretended to be a runner, and raced ahead as I rang my cowbell for her. Not long afterwards, I lay in bed for a nap, thinking about all I had seen, replaying all the interesting, fun and soul-stirring moments again in my mind. As I lay there, I listened to my heart beating, and I felt the fluid in my lungs. I thought about how my life might have been different if I had taken better care of myself. I wondered, "God, how will this turn out?" as I dozed off.

Over a month had passed since the Boston Marathon, and I was still recovering at home; resting, walking and eating as best I knew how. My cardiologist cautioned me to keep my heart rate under 130 beats per minute which, at that time, was a walk with a little extra effort. Tired was the new normal. Moving from bed to computer chair to the dinner table and back to bed was the daily routine, and it took all I had in me to accomplish. The routine was only broken by an occasional walk, or a few minutes in the kitchen preparing something to eat. Thank God the Bruins were in the Stanley Cup finals...it gave me something to do.

I spoke to my case nurse from the insurance company a few times a week, as well as another from the hospital who treated me. They communicated with my primary-care physician, the cardiologist, and eventually a nutritionist. It seemed to me that, with all that assistance, I just wasn't making the kind of progress that I should have been making. I slept a lot. I took short walks and long naps. Eventually, I turned to the internet to see if there was something the doctors were missing; something that I could do to expedite my recovery. The first post I read was in a news group from a 30-something young man that went from an active lifestyle to a similar situation as mine. There were no responses to his post, just his desperate plea to find out what his future held. The *Myocarditis Foundation* said this on their website: "The long-term effects of myocarditis are highly variable. Many people recover heart function without long-term negative health effects and without a return of symptoms (I found, with a little more research, these fortunate souls are young people, even children). In a minority of cases, heart function may not improve after myocarditis (generally older patients), and the individual can require long-term medical therapy and sometimes heart transplantation."

And the internet posts got worse, like this one from StaciStephens.com: "Other than flu-like symptoms immediately preceding Staci's death, there were no outward signs that anything serious was wrong. One thing that we learned after Staci's death was that viral myocarditis has a remarkably high mortality rate. Staci was diagnosed with Coxsackie B..."

Another site said that 33% of patients with this condition die, 33% need heart transplants and 33% have varying stages of recovery. And the American College of Cardiology had this on their site: "our data suggests that patients diagnosed with giant cell myocarditis (or G.C.M., which causes E.K.G. abnormalities and congestive heart failure) who survive more than one year have nearly a 50% combined risk of death, transplantation, ventricular assistance device placement and histologically confirmed disease recurrence. The risk of G.C.M. recurrence continues to at least eight years after diagnosis."

The startling truth was this: no one could tell me how this was going to turn out. There were no tests, and no particular studies that could in any way give me a handle on what to expect. And that was the really hard part - the not knowing, and because of that, hope remained fleeting.

Oh God, what do I do?

CHAPTER FOUR

Good Grief!

According to Elisabeth Kübler-Ross in her 1969 book *On Death and Dying*, terminally ill patients often go through similar emotional stages as they begin to accept that their life is coming to an end (but hopefully, they have an eternal home beyond this life – just a thought). I had a brief brush with the first two stages while I was in the hospital. Both of my parents went through them too, having been diagnosed with cancers that eventually claimed their respective lives. The passage through the end is sad, but I thank God that my parents and I were able to spend some wonderful time together when it counted the most!

Killing off our old lifestyles follows a similar process. When a fatso like me tries to lose weight, they are going to go through similar emotional stages too - lots of them. Like maturing babies, they'll throw a few tantrums along the way!

Stage 1 – Denial: It's not just a river in Egypt! According to the National Heart Lung and Blood Association, if you have a B.M.I. of over twenty-five percent, you are "overweight", and if it is over thirty percent, you are "obese". Not sure what constitutes "husky", "chubby", or "chunky" though. The problem is what you eat; it's not big bones (like your mom always used to tell your aunts and uncles when you were a kid). It's too many calories - it's simple, this isn't rocket science! If you reading this book, you and

DAVID JOHNDROW

I both know why, and it's not to get recipes!

Stage 2 - Anger: I just want to eat what I want, dadgum it! You probably think Jillian Michaels is too skinny, and that guys with six-pack abs got them from sitting around drinking beer watching football. Must be genetic, some folks are just lucky - you? You're not one of the lucky ones, you didn't get them. Hey, I know I get really ticked when I go to lunch with someone my age and they eat an entire freakin' pizza while I limit myself to one or two freakin' slices. You might be mad at God for making everything that tastes so good, be so bad for you, too. Anger, however, is best used as motivation to change (like Ralph Maccio in *The Karate Kid*).

Stage 3 - Bargaining with God: It goes something like this. "Lord if you let me indulge this day and it doesn't show up on the scale, I will give money to the next organization that knocks on my door!" Are you kidding? You popped a pants button and blasted a pigeon right out of the sky. You are a preferred customer at the big and tall store. Nope, bargaining with God just plain doesn't work. Time to get real, and "real" is the root word of reality.

Stage 4 - Depression: Drinking water, putting away the salt shaker, logging your meals, dumping fast food as a dietary option, and - gasp - exercising so that you break a sweat! What a bummer, who wouldn't be depressed?!? It's normal to be bummed out that we can't be like others and eat anything we want, in any quantity we want to.

Stage 5 - Acceptance: Time to snap out it! "It's going to be okay." "I can't fight it, I may as well prepare for it." That's right! Unlike terminal patients, you have a chance to change your history, your health, and your waistline. It's not about what you weigh! It's about the life you lead!

The health benefits of losing weight and keeping it off are amazing. But who cares what your B.M.I. is when you hear a donut calling your name from the break room? If you really accept where you are, you'll stop defending your bad food choices and making excuses for why the scale hates you. Even if your struggle is not specifically with the scale, healthy eating and exercise habits are always a benefit!

Stage 6 - The Afterlife: Terminal patients hopefully get to rest in peace – no more pain, no more suffering. After living in a deteriorating body, it must be a relief. Focusing on what you can do when you lose the weight and get healthy is a good start toward watching the hearse leave your driveway empty. You'll feel better and, for many, depression will be lessened. You'll have better skin, too! You'll be less likely to be sick from viral and bacterial diseases. You'll have more positions you can use for "that." You'll live longer with the ones you love – and maybe even outlive the ones you hate. You'll have more choices for clothing stores. You'll be more comfortable on planes and camel rides. Your joints will feel better. You can eat from the children's menu if you use the curb-side pick up at most of the chains, and that saves money! You'll need less medication when you do need it. You'll have more energy. You'll look younger (unless you are four months old, in which case you probably can't read this anyway). You'll likely have one chin to shave, and not two or three. You'll sleep better. You'll reduce health care costs. You can buy shoes that tie - in fact you might even see your feet for the first time in a long while. You will eventually acquire a taste for what is good for you. You'll put on new underwear and feel like touching yourself (that might just be me), but at least you'll be able to see what you might be touching again.

Getting Your Money's Worth!

If you are like me, once you get started on this journey, you may become a little obsessed with it. I did say, "if you are like me". If I am going to fess up to the calories I eat, I want credit for every darn calorie I burn each day too! Once you make a few sacrifices, like giving up sleeping late to go running at 5:45 am, driving past the fast food joint to go home and cook when you are tired, and picketing bake sales at your child's school, you feel entitled to a reward. I'm sure I'm not unique in this.

We all know that a good long walk, a run, a bicycle ride, a swim, beer and darts (well, the darts anyway), or climbing a mountain, burn calories. Like cheating on a test, I want to get every single calorie on my side of the balance sheet.

It's the little things that add up, laughing for instance. That's right, if you think that a "redneck fire alarm" (Jiffy Pop nailed to the ceiling) on YouTube is funny, you deserve credit for laughing at it (and, by the way, it's hysterical). New research published in the *International Journal of Obesity* has discovered that laughter really is the best medicine for a weight problem. That's right, fifteen minutes a day is ten to fourteen calories.

Not all activity requires you to sweat. Relaxing in fact has its benefits. Look, if you are breathing, you are burning calories! I think this is unfair to us runners, but it's true! If you want lying on the couch to be even more valuable, grab a dumbbell and do some strength weight training, and put on a little muscle while you're at it. The more muscle, the more calories burned.

Another way to burn a few more calories is posing for animal crackers. That's right, standing burns more calories than sitting. So give the world your favorite giraffe pose, and rack up the burn. Or, if you like, the animal crackers could be rewards — strike a pose like an elephant and, if it's a good one, your "trainer" (spouse, child, neighbor with as odd a sense of humor as yours) can toss you a cracker like a fish to a trained seal. Trying to catch it in your mouth burns even more calories! If you play your cards right, your family could charge admission for folks to come in and watch, and you could work up an act like kneeling on the back of the sofa or standing on a giant exercise ball (it'll help cover the overhead costs of the animal crackers).

Sleeping, this is another thing that I am pretty darned good at and, in fact, do a lot of. It has got to count for something, doesn't it? Well, it does. At rest we can burn nearly a thousand calories while dreaming about sitting in a beach chair all day sipping margaritas on a tropical island.

A favorite way to burn a few calories is kissing. I like kissing my kids and my wife (no, not the same way, you pervert!), and apparently the energy it takes to render 9,000 kisses (of either type) add up to a hundred calories!

According to a post on *Healthy Living*, there are at least fifty unusual and surprising ways to burn calories. Cooking, cleaning under the bed and the couch, shopping, and rearranging the furniture are suggestions they offer. I disagree. First, if I am cooking, I am eating, so this is a wash. Shopping? By the time I read the *National Enquirer* and eat the candy I bought while standing in line behind the lady counting out pennies and handing over a train-load of coupons, it's a negative.

Floating Down Denial

You've met them. Some of them are your online friends and others you see face-to-face in real life. They are people who can't see that they are in trouble with their weight, and ultimately their health. And worst of all, you could be one, the one in denial!

You know that you are in denial when:

- You say that, if God had wanted you to exercise and touch your toes, He would have put them higher up on your body.

- Your favorite pants don't fit, and you blame your spouse for washing them in hot water and then drying then on high.

- You go to the coffee shop and tell the cashier the coffee is for you, and the donuts are for your pet fighting fish, when the truth is it's the other way around.

- You go to an "all you can eat" restaurant or buffet because you have invested in their stock.

- You eat whatever you like because you get a lot of exercise - pushing the buttons on the remote.

- You heard that there were two pieces of cake in the fridge, and think how sad it is that you missed one.

- You kick the scale, well, because it's a scale, damn it!

- All your vacation photos at Disney were taken at the Food Court in Epcot Center.

- You get flowers and chocolates from an admirer, and throw the flowers out.

- You eat because, well, your mouth wasn't that busy at the time.

- You are out of breath just thinking about exercise.

- You go to weddings because the cake is free.

- You try to do a push up and discover that a number of body parts never actually leave the floor.

And the last time I rearranged the furniture, I ate two pizzas and drank a liter of cola. And cleaning? I have bad knees, 'nuff said.

Sex! Come on, you already knew this one. One orgasm, two, three or more (clearly, there are some instances when women can lose weight more quickly than men), the details on how much you actually burn are sketchy as even the experts don't agree. Clearly, more testing has to be done on this; you might want to do some of your own to confirm the experts' findings. It is added to my online calorie log as "you know". The automated posts read something like this: "David just did 'you know' for 13 minutes and burned 124 calories and half the house (because he knocked over the candle on the night stand in the process)".

Drinking cold water is touted as a way to burn a few more calories. Apparently if you drink really cold water, your body has to burn calories to warm back up! I am a little confused as to why the same is not true for beer or gin-and-tonics on ice (probably because water, in most municipalities, has no calories). Again, I am not sure the experts agree on how many calories are actually burned, or what the total is if you drink cold water during sex. More testing is needed, obviously.

You Still Don't Want to See Me in a Bikini!

When winter rolls around, New Year's Day comes with it — like it or not. It's the season for hangovers, returning Christmas gifts, and annual resolutions! I remember one New Year's Eve I got into the vodka, and my friend Tomas had to help me get home in the snow; I was sick for three days. I wish that was the last time I did something stupid like that. It took a couple of hundred more tries for me to learn, but today I can say that I have not had a drink in over thirty years. Therefore, I don't make a habit of staying up on New Year's Eve - or any other eve for that matter (whoever Eve might be). I guess it's not the cheesy falling disco ball that makes New Year's worth celebrating. Finishing the shrimp cocktail by nine o'clock is a piece of cake, fending off all of the other party guests is the tough part (did someone mention "cake"?).

In the eighties, I tried to quit smoking cigarettes a number of times. On each attempt, I made it about two or three hours. On one of my more robust endeavors, which lasted almost *twenty-four* hours, my ex-wife bought me a carton of cigarettes and left it with a note: "smoke all these, then call me!" Not being able to stop, I finally went to a healing service and haven't had a cigarette since April fourth, 1994. I remember going with no specific intention of quitting, it just happened, and I just tossed the last pack out of the car window along I-195 on my way home.

New habits often begin with a single decision, changing our behavior is not easy at all. The good news is that success is simply this: don't give up after a failure, but keep on trying until you succeed.

I do believe that most people want the very best for themselves and others. When I struggle with anything in life, I try to put in place some sort of a support network. These are the people that know when I am in trouble; they know what I am going through, and when I am overdoing it. These are the folks that know me best, and that I trust the most, and who won't just let me wander down the wrong road without saying something because they're afraid to hurt my feelings or make me angry. These are folks who won't hesitate to administer a bit of tough-love.

Making friends with people that have lost more weight than I have, or have the same goal as I do, has really helped me. Some of them are virtual in the fitness and running groups I belong to on-line (the good news is that there are no background checks), others are in my run club. I even talked a guy at work into going to the gym with me at lunch.   Reading success stories of others is also inspiring. Every fitness and weight loss site has them. Nothing says it better than before and after pictures! I have seen a trend; most people that are obese, can lose from 40-100 pounds in a year. Think about next year and then get out there for today's workout!

I enjoy a number of inspiring people, but I run with a guy who has lost an excess of 250 pounds. That is almost how much I used to weigh!

Life changes are hard to sustain, but encouraging others can take your mind off of your own progress - or lack thereof. I spend the most time in online communities posting encouragements. I also see plenty of people that need to be encouraged at the gym, running the other way on the street, at run club meetings and people who have come up to me to ask what I did to lose weight.

Everyone approaches fitness, weight loss and exercise differently. One of the things that I have done is log my food using a website. There are a number of them. I don't take days off - I hate to - I even log when I go over, even way over. I logged on the holidays and I logged on vacation. I am initiating a life change. I am done with diets while logging calories reminds me just how fragile this whole thing is. Total honesty is the only way this will work, keeping secrets is a pretty good sign that there is some failure hidden in there.

Taking before and after photos can be very motivating as time progresses. I don't think most people over twenty-two particularly like their photos. It can be an important step, though, as we step through the phases of our fitness development. I am embarrassed about some of the photos that I have shared in this book, and even more so of some that I didn't. The culmination of hard work, time, and the use of some of the knowledge in this book was captured in the portrait I had done for the bio page.

Sharing our experience with others is a good way for us to get a reality check, no matter what is going on in our lives. I write to remind me of what I am up against. Obesity nearly killed me, and exercise saved my life. Dialoging about it helps!

If you can't make a change for just one day, how the hell are you going to do it for a lifetime? I suggest making exercise a daily thing, that way you don't get lost in skipping days. Take it slow; a ten minute walk is better than a can of Pringles.

Working with doctors and nutritionists has been eye-opening, and I am fortunate to have regular blood labs and monthly visits to discuss my food diary with a professional. I also got a personal trainer to make sure that I develop a routine that I can live with. Here is what I found out: all this information is available free online - all of it. So let me save you a few grand: eat lots of fruits, vegetables, low-fat dairy, whole grains, nuts, lean meat, and fish. Do some strength training and get the heart rate up. Schedule your exercise times and stop lying to yourself. There it is, and it only cost you the price of this book (unless you're a cheapskate and you're reading a copy you've borrowed from a friend or snagged off of a coworker's desk).

Another part of my success is drinking water. How much is

enough is a debate that will rage on. I have noticed that fitness geeks and runners discuss pee color like they are a paint salesman at Home Depot. It seems the lighter the shade, the closer you are to the right amount.

There are some constants in life. There are no perfect mates, churches or shortcuts to weight loss. The magic pill that I was looking for doesn't exist. Diet (what you eat, not what you do) and exercise are the only way.

Religion and Politics

It's true, religion and politics can make people emotional. I admit it, I follow politics and I can be very religious – downright ritualistic in fact. If I was warlock, I would have a perfectly organized book of incantations. As magical as that sounds, I am probably more O.C.D. and would actually make a lousy warlock.

As a creature of habit, I like schedules, organization, scientific results and itineraries. My personal calendar includes some of my daily routines to make sure that my life stays changed the way I had changed it. In it will be scheduled my twice-daily blood pressure medication (for my O.C.D.), bimonthly recycling, refuse pick up, date nights, water deliveries, and reminders to pay bills, along with my training schedule, races and family events. I am religious about stuff like that.

I am also religious about using the scale to weigh in. I have a routine that includes some incantations and a blend of prayer and positive thinking. The scale seems to have its own magical powers. For decades I walked past the powerful little package of springs and electronics without a thought. It can make you do the happy dance or make you whimper in defeat. Some call it a scale, others call it a freakin' liar. For weight-losers, it is more coveted than Woody Allen's orgasmatron in the movie *Sleeper*. I have a love/hate relationship with it, and all for good reason; it has become the gauge of our success - or lack thereof.

My youngest daughter was seven at the time of my hospitalization. She would help me answer the automated questions on the "heart program" terminal connected to the scale and blood pressure machine. The first thing that it does is tell me my weight, which used to be 276. One night she said to me, "I don't know where all your fat is, but the lady (voice on the terminal) is still looking for it. Daddy, I don't like your fat."

My twice-daily drink of insanity had mellowed to just getting bombed on the weekend. It's like playing the roulette wheel as the adrenaline begins to flow. Honestly, how sick is that? Medical advice started my addiction after my heart failure back in April of 2011. The doctors had me weighing in two times a day along with taking a handful of prescription medications. After a while, it was hard to walk by the black box without stepping on it. Like a heroin addict, I started out with the fantasy of a score. Just the thought of a pound or two lost caused my heart to race. Just a side note: I don't know why I don't feel this way taking out the trash on Wednesday evenings. I guess I have some soul-searching to do.

The stroll to the bathroom has my mind racing with the pre-flight liturgy. Topping the checklist is going number one. Except giving a urine sample with the attending health care worker waiting outside the paper thin door, this is never a problem. Going number two, that is more of a project, but, scientifically speaking, because we eat every day, we should always have one in the chamber.

Murphy's Law states that the batteries in the scale must fail during the pre-hurricane or pre-blizzard rush at the hardware store. Fresh batteries provide consistent results unless you have a mechanical scale. If you must weight in, they have mechanical ones at the YMCA. From experience, I do not recommend using the hanging one in the produce aisle. I can tell you that it took real effort and contortions to get into that metal scoop, and it took two good-sized store security officers to get me out (obviously, I don't shop there any more).

Planning the big meeting with Mr. Scale is best done in the morning. The body gains weight throughout the day as you eat. It can be as much as five or six pounds (two to three kilos) of extra weight. For the best results, before breakfast is usually the best time. Whatever time of day you choose, remember to be consistent by weighing in on the same day and the same time each week. Look, we all want to have those scale victories, but not weighing in because you had a bad food day or a pimple or whatever, is not a reasonable excuse.

Excuses Can Kill You

I used a whole bunch excuses for ending up feeling miserable as I lay on the couch. And now that I have finally found my way out, I hear a fair amount of them from others. Here are some common ones debunked.

I Have Slow Metabolism: Right, and if your body was a car, it would be in reverse. Personally, mine hit a speed bump at age forty and broke the steering column.

My Parents Didn't Teach me How to Eat: Are you kidding, have you looked in the mirror? You are probably very good at eating, in fact exceptional. For God's sake, birds manage to find their way south.

It's the Holidays! The Bermuda Triangle: Thanksgiving, Christmas and New Year's. (Or Memorial Day, the 4th of July and Labor Day.) Flag Day, the dog's birthday, there are lots of holidays, just pick one!

It's Vacation: One of my personal favorites, lots of eating out and lying around (actually that sounds more like work). Staying in the hospital is not a vacation.

I Don't Like Healthy Food: Let me know when the pity party is over. Trust me, you are not going to like heart failure either.

It's Emotional: Huh? It's food, get over it.

I Can Eat Anything I Want! Apparently!

I'll Start Over Tomorrow: Well, now tomorrow is today, now what?

Water Makes Me Gag! It's a good thing you are not a dolphin, I guess.

I Have Bad Knees (bad ankles, bad hips, etc.): From here it looks like they can get you back and forth from the store, the bathroom and the refrigerator.

If you need an edge to get you down an ounce or two, think body fluids. Yep, if you are desperate for a loss, clean your ears, blow your nose, and spit - might as well get a haircut and clip your nails too. Then take a hot shower (a least once a week) to rinse off all of those loose epithelials. You may even sweat a few ounces off, and at the very least, you'll feel better.

Dressing for the occasion is important! Obviously naked is the best - well as long as you are not using the gym scale in the workout room. Try to wear the same exact same thing each time. And finally, weigh in post-workout if you have one in the morning. You'll sweat during your workout, so why not take advantage of it.

Another great idea is to use a tape measure. Often when we get started exercising, we not only burn some fat, but we build muscle, which offsets our losses. The good news is that our proportions begin to change in that process. Remember, the scale can be a demon and the tape is not a poisonous snake. Be sure to take all your measurements each month. And when the scale doesn't budge, you'll have victory anyway! If you are new, remember that circuit training can add three to ten pounds of muscle in a few short months, especially the first month! The muscle, according to experts, acts like a sponge and retains water - as much as five to possibly even ten pounds! Don't be discouraged with the scale, but enjoy the victories of the tape measure.

Look, there is no substitute for regular exercise and a healthy diet (what you eat, not what you do). If you can make the time to do at least twenty minutes of brisk walking, jogging, running or biking, and ten minutes of strength training three times each week, along with watching the calories, you'll be amazed at how kind the scale can be to you.

Remember, if you are overweight or obese, food retention is your problem (calories consumed)!

CHAPTER FIVE

Faith Healing

It's not just what you put in your mouth that makes you fat. Most people think the problem with obese people is what they eat, and in a few cases that may be true, but it's far more important what comes out your mouth! It was once written, "as a man thinketh in his heart, so is he..." (or she).

Spending time in an online weight loss and fitness community, I began to notice what people were saying, whether in seriousness or in jest, which reflects their attitudes toward weight loss. A negative self-image is as damaging as a conceited and boastful Rod Stewart singing "Do you Think I'm Sexy?" What comes from our self-talk eventually crosses our tongue. Here are some of the things I've heard.

I'm Too Fat: That's right, it may be a fact that you are fat, overweight or even obese like I was, but that is not the attitude of a weight-loser! Have you ever thought that you are a skinny person having a fat moment? The time has come to make better choices in life, in relationships, and certainly in food. Skinny people make good food and exercise choices, and so can you. Try saying this: "I am getting thinner!"

I Can't Lose Weight: My answer is, you are correct, not with an attitude like that! For some of us it's freakin' *hard* to do too. I mean I trip skinny people on the escalator in the mall because I am so jealous! (There's a certain satisfaction in that, but I'm not advocating violence here.) The truth is that I *could* lose weight, and I *did*! Try saying this: "I *am* losing weight!"

Food is My Weakness: No, your lifestyle is your weakness. Set your life up to succeed. Though I have occasionally heard them whispering my name, I have never been mugged by a stack of pancakes or a chocolate cake! Try saying this: "I have a new lifestyle."

I'm Losing Weight For _____: Lots of answers for that one: for my wedding, for bikini season, to get a girlfriend, so I don't get harpooned at the beach... WRONG! WRONG! WRONG! What happens when your event passes, the winter comes, or the whaleboat sails off to deeper water? Then your weight loss goal goes away and with it, your motivation. Instead, you need to be changing your lifestyle so that you'll be healthy. Maybe you need a tour to the local Intensive Care Unit to receive your wake-up call? Scared straight, as it were. Having lost about thirty pounds prior to my heart trauma not only saved my life, but it screwed my wife out of a huge life insurance settlement. Try saying this: "I am getting *healthy*, and losing weight is part of my success!"

I'll Get Back on Track Tomorrow: Which tomorrow? How many of those have passed? All you have for sure is today and hey, sometimes today feels like someone wrenched out a nose hair with pliers (aaaauuugh!). So what? You got off track with the first purchase of unhealthy food, or subjecting yourself to places where it is available. Here's a tip, try planning your food choices before the days starts to see where you'll end up. This is especially true if you are planning to go to a restaurant. Check the menu online first! Try saying this: "Today I am making good food and exercise choices."

I Know, My Friend Says I Am a Nut

May eighth, 2011, I got up and was heading for the YMCA to do my triweekly mile on the treadmill. It was five minutes to nine, the Mother's Day breakfast in bed for my wife had been a success, and I wanted to get to the local church for the 10:30 service. I heard the Lord prompt me, "go to the 9:00 service." I know that somehow hearing from God makes me a whack job to some folks, but it was just a sense I had — a feeling — a deep impression that somehow needed to be listened to, not an audible voice speaking to me. I swapped my red and black striped workout pants for a pair of blue jeans and headed to the Vineyard Christian Fellowship near my home.

There was a time, a number of years earlier, when I regularly attended this church. It might seem odd, but I didn't really feel welcomed there. The reality was that driving long distances was too risky since my stay in the I.C.U. At times I would just feel incredibly tired and need a nap, and most folks frown on you for doing that during a service — especially if you tend to snore.

The little church was a storefront between an Indian grocery and a traditional Jewish delicatessen; you could get a kosher tongue sandwich on rye and walk just two doors down for some saffron and curry (I love America). Only about twenty people were in attendance that morning in a very plain room with a couple of large-screen monitors on the walls bracketing an acoustic quartet and a simple music stand pulpit. I made my way to an empty section on the far side of the room. I sat through the acoustic worship set which was followed by a sermon on forgiveness — "Dropping the F-Bomb" it was entitled — both were introspective.

Photo by Zoe Johndrow

June 19, 2011

I got to celebrate Father's Day, and all the girls were there. I had a chance to enjoy my wife for a few minutes, too. I felt lighter – I was down to 217 pounds. And just to make my Father's Day complete, the Bruins won the Stanley Cup against the Canucks.

After the service I was in the lobby chatting over a cup of coffee with an old acquaintance which, at one time, I had played with on the worship team. Quietly, one of the pastors interrupted us and mentioned that Pat, one of the elders, had just given a word of knowledge. "There is someone here this morning with a weak heart, and I believe God wants to heal it."

On a dark Wednesday evening in the winter of 2011, I was about to teach my first small group personal training class — ever — at the Metrowest YMCA in Framingham, Massachusetts. There was a man, a talkative man, who was the first to arrive and check in. His name was David Johndrow.

David had a list of physical ailments including a bum shoulder, an arthritic back and knees, but most severe, was congestive heart failure. I was immediately overwhelmed because I had never worked with anyone with cardiac issues before. Because he produced the prerequisite forms and completed his PAR-Q (a release form from his cardiologist), there was no reason for me to exclude him.

As I checked in other participants, he quickly made friends with the other team members. We began with a light warm up — some jumping jacks, squats and lunges. David never complained, but never stopped talking either. He quickly gained a reputation as the class smart-ass. He shared his story and was an inspiration for everyone in that group, so much so, that the entire group signed up for the next eight-week session!

David never said no to an exercise I suggested. He plowed his way through kettle bell, medicine balls, BOSU ball routines, burpees, superman's, squats, lunges, rope climbs and every ab exercise I know. He did this all in the first three weeks of classes.

In challenging the group to run a road race that he had registered for, David recruited me and two other participants in the class to run our very first race, the "Run with Heart 5k" in Clinton, Massachusetts. He did really well, and I was so proud of my student.

As the winter turned into spring, David continued to lose weight, but more importantly became much more physically fit. He recruited some of our new group members, and together we ran two more races. He hasn't stopped running since, and I know he has plans to run a full marathon; and he never forgets to remind me that he will beat me, which keeps me running, too.

His journey is one that is truly inspirational, truly motivating, and should be shared with as many people as possible. I couldn't be more inspired and honored to have been a part of his incredible journey.

— Cherilynn Blumenthal, NASM-CPT, FNS

Cherilynn is a certified personal trainer and fitness nutrition specialist through the National Academy of Sport Medicine. She enjoys running and taking part in obstacle course races. She hopes one day to run the Boston Marathon and beat David's time.

She said, "Maybe you should get prayer?" I didn't know where to go, so I went back into the sanctuary with another fellow named Don. Pat greeted me and asked me about my heart condition. After a very brief conversation, we agreed, certainly my heart was weak. He gently laid his hand on my shoulder and said a simple prayer — nothing fancy or King James-like. I thought, "does God have a plan for David this morning?" The pleasant spring weather was hinting that summer was not far off. For the first time since I was in the hospital, the warmth of the sunshine felt good as I started my car to go home. In fact, it was so nice I decided to take a little drive.

Wednesday morning I sat in the cardiologist's office for my six-week check up. My wife came with me to the exam room to ask questions and help me to make sure I heard what the doctor said (some of the medications I was taking had the side effect of confusion). For me, the medication only exacerbated a pre-existing condition! The nursing staff stuck E.K.G. pads to my body which was easier now because I had had so many of them adhered to me while I was in the hospital, that there was no chest or leg hair left to be pulled out.

I could hear the nurse whispering to an aide. "Oh my God!" Of course I thought something was wrong. I looked at my wife, but she wasn't sure what was going on either. I was afraid things were getting worse. I later found out that she had been comparing my E.K.G. from this visit to the one when I was admitted to the I.C.U. a few weeks earlier. There was a drastic difference the cardiologist told me! He later confirmed it with my echo-cardiogram the next week saying that my heart function was now completely normal! He took me off all the medications except for the one I had been taking for high blood pressure.

I confess, although he was very pleased that both the E.K.G. and subsequent ultrasound were fine, I still didn't feel very energetic — not that I felt super energetic before, but I still didn't feel like I did before the heart trauma. According to the doctor, this was as good as it gets – or at least a lot better than most. Actually I started to think he didn't believe me that I used to feel better than I did then. To make my emotional state worse, there were those words I had read online, "most people who suffer this condition live five-to-ten years. 33% of the people that have a myocarditis die, 33% need a heart transplant, and the rest have varying degrees of recovery". I just didn't want to accept that this was as good as it gets. I was depressed. I had read about the emotions that people who have had heart attacks go through and I was experiencing all of them. I did my best not to be discouraged and started running again. It was just the first week of a program called Couch to 5K (C25K), but I was doing it. I also had to keep my heart rate under 140 beats per minute, so I was slow, very slow.

Another Speed Bump

Not long after the good news about my heart, I found a lump in my shorts, not the one I was familiar with. I called my primary care physician and made an appointment. I had had so many exams in the previous few weeks, I stopped wearing underwear to take off during them. After a close inspection, he ordered an ultrasound.

I headed over to the radiology lab. (If you are listening to this on audio book, you may want to use headphones or remove small children from the room.) Into the "Johnny" I went...again. I honestly had thought about purchasing one of my own to wear under my t-shirt and jeans, just to streamline this all-too-routine process.

I don't know who the perfect ultrasound tech would have been. I guess I was expecting an understanding older woman or a middle-aged guy who decided he couldn't make enough to support his family changing oil at Jiffy Lube. As luck would have it, I got an attractive, articulate young woman who greeted me and proceeded to hike up my bed clothes. I sort of hung onto the sheet and we had a tug-of-war. Finally I gave up and a blast of cool air wafted over my privates as they went into full retreat. Although she surveyed the situation without laughing, I still wasn't exactly at ease. "I am just going to put on some ultrasound cream," she said. "It's a little cold."

"I thought they warmed it up?!" I said in a scared little girly voice.

"They used to until they found out that it caused bacterial formations." She replied in a very professional voice.

"I have been exposed to plenty of bacteria, and I am sure by now I'm immune to it."

Again she smiled. I closed my eyes while in my mind's eye I pictured frost on an October pumpkin. I squirmed a little as I gritted my teeth. I tried to pray, but I couldn't get past, "forgive me Father, for I have sinned."

What happened next is none of your business.

Finally she said, "you are all set, and you can get dressed. Your doctor will call you with the results."

"Thank you."

As I started to get dressed, I couldn't help but wonder just how much more friggin' embarrassing could all this get? I looked around for my underwear until I finally remembered that I didn't have any. I stood naked for a few minutes while I checked my email and Facebook. I pulled on my jeans and t-shirt and looked at the floor as I walked past the staff at the nurse's station. I was hoping that they wouldn't say anything. Fortunately they were true professionals.

Humility — perhaps the hardest lesson of all in this journey.

CHAPTER SIX

Running for My Life

A Day at the Gym with a Nerd

Non-scale victories (NSV) are actually more important than the ones on the scale - presuming you lose enough weight in the right places to make a difference. Today I have to admit, they are not always comfortable. Five or six months into my journey, I went out and bought some new clothes. Essential fact of life: men abhor shopping for clothes. We'd rather go for root canal without anesthesia while being forced to watch Ellen DeGeneres on a TV with bad reception. You may have heard about me in line at airport security, I'm kind of a legend at Logan. Long story short: Good morning, Boston!

If size matters, here is another NSV: I went from wearing XXL shirts to Large (or "grande" if you pressed button number one). For a little more comfort in the gym, I still wear an XL. Actually I am just cheap, and why get a nice new t-shirt all stinky? I have also been keeping up with my underwear collection ever since my hospitalization back in April. I decided not to go "commando" just in case. God knows, I have had more health care workers view the unmentionables than any other people group on Earth; the only possible exception being the passengers on flight 1024 to San Francisco (see chapter 7), another wardrobe malfunction legend.

At our YMCA, people pretty much dress like they are going to Wal-Mart followed by a dump run on Saturday morning. In spite of feeling the need to wear old t-shirts and torn sweat pants, or (shudder) spandex, I got a couple of spiffy new training suits. I began to feel better about myself, and the old horn rims from the sixties weren't doing it for me any more - or anyone else I know (I'm no Drew Carey). So I also bought a stylishly-new pair of glasses. I am pretty comfortable with the David inside (read: perfect in my own eyes - right?), so I thought I should like the outside just as much.

The day after my shopping spree, I got home and went to my room to change in to my new gym "stuff". I am guy, so I took a moment to admire my new underwear in the mirror (these special moments don't come along all that often in a guy's life). Then I sucked it in, and bent my arm in a bicep pose for the audience in my mind's eye - was that a snicker I heard from the hallway? Nope, nobody there.

I pulled on my new sweats, a t-shirt and a training jacket. I shoved my cell phone, my car keys with a gym pass and my wallet into the front pockets, tied my sneakers (no longer having to gasp for air to do that), and bounced downstairs and out the door to the car. It's amazing what new underwear will do for a man!

I parked at the "Y", put on my headphones, and made my way to the door under the street lights. Bouncing up a few more stairs, I shoved my pass in front of the scanner. I was very much enjoying my musical cocoon as I rocked out to a CD I recorded with a friend. I walked in to the workout room with my head swaying to the rhythm. As I passed the floor-to-ceiling-mirror, I got a glimpse of what I first thought was a stranger. Then I realized it was my own reflection. I let out a little girly scream, and my man-card fell off my key ring! I had forgotten to take the sales tags off my new duds. I was rockin' Minnie Pearl and didn't even know it (thank God I left the hat at home). So, I pretended to trip, and tore the tags from the jacket, making a coughing sound to mask the sound of the strings snapping and the adhesive peeling away. I stood up looking as normal as someone like myself can. Then nonchalantly, I dropped them in trash. I thought: I hope no one has my fingerprints.

When you are wearing headphones, it's hard to know what people saw. I circled back pretending to look disgusted, like someone had taken my favorite treadmill, and stepped in front of the mirrors again.

Hmm...

I hung up my jacket and headed for the treadmill. As I punched in data for my run, one of the trainers that I had for a weight loss class back when I started, came over to say how good I looked after losing all that weight.

I replied, "Thank you, I have new underwear on."

Out the Door I Went

My treadmill runs were getting boring, so I decided to brave the New England elements and run in my own neighborhood.

I am usually up around 5:45 each morning, head on downstairs, switch on the PC in the office, make my way to the kitchen for the first of my daily cups-o-joe, let the dogs out while it brews, and head back to the keyboard to check my email, Facebook, log my blood pressure, and get ready to work on my Couch To 5k program. It's the same each day - my formula for getting the day kick-started. It's pretty rigid and very religious without being obsessive. Having suffered a heart trauma five months before, I was grateful for the simple things, still am. Mostly I'm grateful for not being in the hospital and being able to get out for some fresh air. It had been a struggle to that point, but I was back to work part-time by then, and feeling better. Although I was previously exercising regularly, I wasn't as serious about it as I had become after being sick.

I like to run outside as often as I can. We did get eighty-eight inches of snow in the months just before I got sick. I had been using the gym since that February, which is a good option during the winter months, and the treadmills are wide enough for snowshoes - just in case. As spring became summer, I found it best to run early when it's cooler. That, and I only have to take one shower a day (being very green to be saving water like that). The crosswalk gods were good to me too, as they were freshly painted.

The podiatrist insisted that I walk before I run, so I fiddled with my smartphone as I headed out of the neighborhood. Sometimes, when I'd get to the end of the block, I'd still be half asleep. My trusty Android watches my heart rate, counts my steps, averages my pace, monitors my speed and route and plays a custom play list of "running" tunes such as: "Take the Money and Run" by Steve Miller, "Born to Be Wild" from the sixties band Steppenwolf, "Set Me on Fire" performed by Burn Service, "Born to Run" from the Boss, and "Turn it Around" by Israel Houghton and New Breed, along with similar rock and worship tunes. The music can really set the pace; therefore wimpy slow stuff is out!

I'd pass by Gleason Pond, watching the swans about the same time Noom would tell me that I had just completed three-tenths of a mile. On occasion, I'd see a blue heron fishing among the lily pads. As I'd pick up the pace, jogging a few more blocks to warm up, I would decide on a route for the morning. I had four regular routes with the shortest being about a mile and a half, and the longest being closer to four miles. I liked the one with the steady half mile slope that passes by Massachusetts Bay College the best, although I would run it backwards on occasion (that is, run the route backwards, not run backwards, lest I crash into a wayward swan).

A mile in, I'd check my time to see where I was. My stamina was good for longer, but my knee (a touch of runner's knee due to not warming up!) and the fact that I needed to get to work, would push or pull the pace for the second mile.

Adjusting the tempo of sneaker-to-pavement, I have certain songs that make me want to pray as I run, so I do. Huffing-and-puffing my way down the sidewalk, I didn't get to get too religious in my prayers, zipping by the scenery at six-and-a-half miles per hour. I would just ask, and move on to the next item on my list. I don't recommend this as a regular way of praying, but some of the music just sort of lent itself to certain prayers.

I would pass a few other runners from the National Guard Armory. Those guys really move! There are a couple of other faces that give a quick smile or slight wave as they pass in the other direction, fumbling with their iPods. On the lawn at the school, I'd often see a few folks practicing Tai Chi at 6:30 AM. It would give me pause to wonder about what one does in Tai Chi that might connect them with God. I guess it seemed a little religious to me as I was praying - ha!

Like a little city, dozens of squirrels amused themselves beneath the oak trees, gathering acorns and eating breakfast. As I'd round the corner and head down the hill toward the lake, I could see the hospital where I was in I.C.U. just a few short months before. I would muse about how many thousands of beats my heart has made since that day. I thanked God for them.

To this day, I am glad that I had good care, insurance, and have had an excellent recovery. Many who have suffered with Viral Myocarditis don't. I often think about folks who rely solely on what the insurance company or the government can provide for them. I also joyously rely on my faith.

Pouring on the speed for the last half-mile, I would start thinking about getting home, getting a lunch made for later, grabbing a shower, and then heading off to work in rush hour traffic. I would walk past the last two houses to my front door, often wishing I had the time and stamina to go longer. Certainly not working would help, and so would feeling better.

More Love, More Power

I continued to work on my walk/run intervals and struggled with Couch To 5k. I had to repeat a lot of weeks in the program. During that time I continued to complain to the nurses who were working my case, my primary care physician and other people that I knew in health care. I was still sleeping ten hours a day or more. The cardiologist ordered a sleep study. The P.C.P. gave a battery of blood tests and finally sent me to see an immunologist. The specialist interviewed me about everything from my diet history to my sex life (I confess there was a time when they were the same). He wanted to know what brands and types of food I ate, as well as a complete medical history including every head cold I had ever had. Finally he sent me down to the lab for more blood tests.

The tests came back positive for two viruses: Coxsackie B was the one most likely responsible for the Myocarditis. The bad news, there was nothing they could do for me. There was no treatment, no medicine - nothing but time. "It will take nine to twelve months for this to clear up," the immunologist told me. "We will re-test every forty-five days."

Well, at least I finally had some sort of an answer, or so I thought.

One Sunday I came back from my run/walk around the neighborhood. It was about 8:00 AM and I heard that voice again. "David I want you to go to the church in New Hampshire where your brother goes."

"But that's two hours away," I thought. At that stage of my slow recovery progress, I was still a little concerned about a two-hour drive, but I got dressed and climbed in the car.

I arrived at the little country church in New Hampshire a few minutes before the service started. I had never been there before. It was just a simple building with a short white steeple. "What am I doing here?" I thought. Don't get me wrong, I was glad to be there, but I had no idea what was going on. It just seemed a little odd to me. They were having some big name speaker or something, and I sat in folding chairs with my brother's family not far from the front. I started thinking I would get too tired on the drive back, and was getting a little anxious.

The speaker, Wayne Anderson, stepped to the podium, or whatever they call it there. I had heard him speak ten or twelve years earlier, but it wasn't anything special or memorable (might have been my age, too). Right off, he announced, "before I get started I would like to pray for someone." He then walked over and laid a hand on my shoulder and said, "I don't know what you have, but I curse whatever blood disease you have, in the name of Jesus." Then he walked back to the podium and gave his message.

I don't remember what his message was that morning. I didn't feel anything on my shoulder in particular except a little warmth from his hand. I had lunch with my brother and his family, and then drove home to Massachusetts. All I could think of was how did he know I was sick? How did that elder at the other church know there was someone with a weak heart? God, what is going on? I kept trying to connect the dots.

Wednesday that next week, I had another blood test, it had been forty-five days. I never gave the incident at the church another thought. I just keep taking care of myself, running, eating, resting and showing up for exams with no underwear. On Saturday morning I got a call from the immunologist while I was grocery shopping. "Your tests came back completely negative," He said. "Everything is fine. I don't need to see you anymore. Do you have any questions?"

Was he serious? I didn't know what to say, so I thanked him

and finished unloading my shopping cart.

Not long after that, I went for my six-month check up with the cardiologist and had another echo cardiogram. The doctor said, "not only is your heart completely normal and stronger than last time, but it's like it never happened!"

I might be a wack-job, but this was good news; in fact, it doesn't get any better. A few weeks later I returned to work full time. Even better, the cardiologist lifted the heart rate cap of 150 beats per minute. To celebrate, I took off my heart monitor and went for a run.

Running

Running was becoming more and more of a reality, and I loved it. I would go out early in the morning and walk for a few minutes, and then jog up the hill past the pond. It was the only real peace that I had. Being out of work due to my illness, and living on one-forth of my regular salary had made lots to things difficult, and others quite stressful. I had a 1.8 mile loop around the neighborhood which I was going to expand to a 5K run with a few modifications. One day I had a brilliant idea - the secret to a fast time - I decided to run down the biggest hill in the city. I headed over to Dennison Street. Oh, that hurt. I was sore for a few days.

As night became morning, I went for a run. Like most new runners, I was allergic to rain. Outside, a very light sprinkle fell on fall's first fallen leaves. I'll be back in twenty minutes, I thought, so I headed out. As I was running up the hill near the pond, I slipped on some wet leaves. I had a sharp pain in my right knee. I thought, I will just walk it off. I kept going, but by the time I was done, I was badly in need of ice and a few Motrin tablets.

I took a few more days off, but when I ran, it hurt. Every day I would come home from my little loop and put ice on it, elevate it, and take a couple of Motrin. I kept thinking that I could out-run the pain. I even had a six-minute and fifty-seven second mile (in high school it was 6:10)! Finally, the aging knee needed the attention of a real doctor – an orthopedic surgeon.

He told me to ride the bike for four weeks and come back to see him. Riding bikes in metro Boston is near suicide. You aren't allowed on the sidewalk, and you are not wanted on the road. You are precariously perched somewhere between a car bumper and the asphalt, madly pedaling like a Kamikaze, hoping that people in parked cars along the way will see you coming, and don't their doors open as you approach. It's truly a religious experience.

I followed the doctor's instructions, and I began to feel alright. After a month, I went back and he released me to run a little, a few times a week. I had a problem right away. I hadn't done "a little" of anything (except tofu) in my life. Running was bearable, but not the kind that I wanted to do. I was hoping to finish Couch To 5k; it had been almost a year since I had first started.

CHAPTER SEVEN

Snakes on a Plane

Flying to California, I had finished the first leg of my journey, and had also just finished browsing through the *History Of TV* exhibit at the San Francisco International Airport on my way to pick up my suitcase and secure a rental car. I hadn't flown in over five years, and I almost want to say that I didn't miss it. Travel used to be such a wonderful adventure, but it had turned into a bothersome tangle of frenetic rules and mayhem. As an ex-travel writer and clueless vagabond, there was a love/hate battle going on in my brain. I've flown so much; I would be hard-pressed to count the number of times I have been in the air. Air travel can be boring until I look out the window and see the Rockies from 30,000 feet! Those moments kind of make up for all the frenetics.

That particular journey started at 4:45 AM that morning. I had gotten up to get a coffee, checked My Fitness Pal, Facebook, Twitter, and pulled myself together for a cold morning ride to Boston's Logan Airport. My wife and youngest daughter dropped me off in front of Terminal C; I was supposed to be at A. Thanks to the MBTA for their out-of-date website. Next time, guys, call me - that is what I do for a living! I got a complimentary shuttle to A from C, completing my algebraic introduction to the new age of we-charge-for-friggin'-everything type flying. Two bucks to tip the shuttle driver who squashed the foot of a traveller who was stupidly on foot. Hopefully they'd learned their lesson, next time they will take the shuttle (some of those MBTA drivers find visual aids much more effective than profanity). Then on to the check-in, where I paid another twenty-five dollars for a piece of crap suitcase filled with clothes that no longer fit.

I stood in line playing with my smartphone while I waited for security. I really liked John, one of the pre-screeners. If everyone in Boston was like him, Massachusetts would become a red state. I didn't get John; I got Bob (a.k.a. "Boris"), who was obviously an ex-KGB agent, burned-out and surly at the end of his twenty-four-hour shift.

"Well David, we'd like to ask you a few security questions", he said as he looked at my driver's license. "Dang, you don't look like you weigh 275, sir."

"I don't any longer."

"Why does it say that on your license?"

"Well, I used to weigh that much, but I have lost weight." I said with a proud smirk.

I was wondering if these were the security questions - and if he'd asked me how I did it, I was going to say that I had a kidney stone removed by a falling meteor that came through the ceiling one night. But then I remembered: these guys are devoid of humor, probably best to just keep the sarcasm to myself.

"What's your final destination, sir?"

"Redding, California."

"What are you going to do there?"

"I'm attending a conference."

"How'd you lose all the weight?"

"MFP." (My Fitness Pal) I replied.

"Have a good day."

That was it? Whew!

I got into the line to take off my shoes and put my junk in a tub to be x–rayed. "Can you take off your belt and put your laptop through separately." said the attendant.

I froze. I thought, "I am going to end up with the FBI and the TSA grilling me in a dark little room as my way-too-big pants drop the floor without the support of a belt.

I uttered the words, "I can't" under my breath, as I weighed the consequences of not complying. You see, I was wearing an old pair of jeans with a forty-inch waistband, but by then I was normally wearing a thirty-four. I needed my belt, but I took it off anyway and placed it in the gray tub. I stepped into the full body scanner, grasping a belt loop to avoid a very ugly incident.

"Sir, can you place your hands above your head?" The screener asked as she pointed to the diagram In front of me.

"Oh God save me," I whispered.

A few seconds later, I heard the little girl standing in line behind me ask her father, "What's Calvin Klein, Daddy?"

As I stood there waiting to get my belt back, I heard one the TSA agents says, "I think he's got something in his rectum." I knew I shouldn't have eaten that Tabouli salad!

West Coast Wobble

It had been seven months since I was admitted to the intensive care unit in Boston. I had arrived two days before the conference started, so I could relax. It was a much-needed oasis. I drove through the mountains of northern California to the coast and visited Redwoods National Park. I hiked five or six miles that day, but then I needed to give my knee a rest, and take some Motrin to ease the pain. It was the same a few days later at Shasta Dam. I walked across and back, and sat in my car icing my right knee with some crushed ice I got from the snack bar. There was no running, no biking and the nagging feeling that I would need to see the surgeon when I got home grew in my mind.

After the conference, my family arrived and we took a few days to visit Yosemite, Sanoma Valley, San Francisco, and to drive along the coast. It was magnificent!

It's hard to come home after a vacation, especially a great one like that. And even more difficult was admitting defeat - the knee was not getting better. Four weeks on the bicycle and four weeks without running was all I could take. At the surgeon's office they took more x-rays and did another exam. Then he ordered an M.R.I.

Classic Rock was no help, the M.R.I. tube is just too small for comfort. The video clips confirmed everyone's suspicions: I had a torn meniscus which would need repair. While they were in there, they were going to take care of some arthritis too (no extra charge

- are you kidding?). Checking out of the doctor's office, the receptionist and I scheduled a pre-op exam and a surgery date. On the way home I was a little frightened, a little depressed, and painfully discouraged. I had lost nearly forty pounds since I began my journey. Now I wanted to run. I just hoped that the surgery would be a cure. Nothing I read online helped build my confidence, and the doctor only seemed to think a few miles a week were ultimately going to be possible.

Without running, I didn't know what I was going to do. Biking in the city wasn't particularly safe, swimming would be great if you can find the time (and know how to swim), and there just didn't seem to be anything else that would be easy, inexpensive, and simple to add to a busy schedule.

The Effects of Vicodin, Dec 8, 2011

On December eighth, 2011, barely eight months after being in the I.C.U., the cardiologist cleared me for knee surgery. Because I am so technologically savvy, I decided to "tweet" the entire event, knowing how entertaining it would be for all my friends. Once the drug Versed kicked in, I lost track of the difference between "sharing what's on my mind", and "should I talk to a therapist about this". Had you been one of my followers on Twitter that day, here's the feed. (Actually Nurse Cratchet took away my smartphone. Here is what I would have said in 140 characters or less.)

5:15 am I.C.U.2Marathon: Up, no coffee, no breakfast, weigh in, blood pressure 131/82. Time for a shower. No coffee! #RatherBeInBed

5:16 am I.C.U.2Marathon: No coffee, no damn coffee! #NeedCoffee

5:16 am I.C.U.2Marathon: No coffee, just no damn coffee! #INeedTheDamnCoffee

5:44 am I.C.U.2Marathon: Kissed Mary Anne and sleeping Charlotte goodbye. :(#SadDay

5:45 am I.C.U.2Marathon: Jot is here to take me to the hospital.

5:46 am I.C.U.2Marathon: That coffee smells good, Jot. #INeedTheEffingCoffee

5:50 am I.C.U.2Marathon: Jot's retired and he told me all about his new Medicaid benefits. #SmallTalk

5:55 am I.C.U.2Marathon: Jot prayed for my surgery. He knows a lot about this having done it himself. #PrayerIsGood

5:59 am I.C.U.2Marathon: Making my way to Surgical Day Care. A little anxious. Thinking "doggie day care" for some reason.

6:00 am I.C.U.2Marathon: Answering identity questions for the admitting nurse. Thinking about COFFEE! What is this the TSA? #Interrogations

6:05 am I.C.U.2Marathon: Shown to my cube - almost like work except a bed instead of a desk. Hmm... new office arrangement? #NotWorking

6:06 am I.C.U.2Marathon: WTF! Take off everything? How about I keep my underwear? #DignityGone

6:10 am I.C.U.2Marathon: Right, just a little pinch. How come there is blood squirting everywhere? That's good stuff, don't waste any! #NothingButTheBlood

6:15 am I.C.U.2Marathon: I'm going to have to log the IV, how many calories are in the stuff? #MyFitnessPalGuilt

6:16 am I.C.U.2Marathon: Can you put coffee in that? #INeedTheEffingCoffee

6:25 am I.C.U.2Marathon: Talked to the anesthesiologist. I chose one of each from the menu! #LoveTheDrugs

6:30 am I.C.U.2Marathon: Talked to the OR nurse and chose my music. #ClassicRock #WhyDoWeNeedMusic

6:40 am I.C.U.2Marathon: Was relieved the nurse decided to shave me with a clipper. When I saw that roll of tape it made my navel pucker. #HolyCrap

6:50 am I.C.U.2Marathon: Doc in. Initialed my right leg. Borrowed his Sharpie and wrote "NOT THIS ONE!" on my left. Doc not impressed. #DumbMove

7:00 am I.C.U.2Marathon: In the OR now, praying #PrayerIsGood, oxygen and Lidocane. Smells fun.... #OutLikeALight

7:05 am I.C.U.2Marathon: Why are you painting my leg red? Purple is my favorite color. #HallucinationsAreInteresting

7:15 am I.C.U.2Marathon: What are you doing with the thing? I wish I had my underwear! #FearOfAwesomeMedicalDevices

7:20 am I.C.U.2Marathon: OR TV? I hate *The View*, can you change it to the NHL Channel? #NHL

7:22 am I.C.U.2Marathon: Is that Barbara Walters on skates? #HallucinationsAreInteresting

7:25 am I.C.U.2Marathon: Are you Santa Clause? I have been very good this year. #BeenGoodAllYear #HallucinationsAreInteresting

7:45 am I.C.U.2Marathon: Ahhhh! It is Santa Clause, my parents lied! #Fear #SantasNotReal

8:15 am I.C.U.2Marathon: Did fine, in recovery. They have Fentanyl. I like that better than coffee. #LoveTheDrugs #CoffeeIsOverated

8:30 am I.C.U.2Marathon: Mary Anne is here, everything is OK. #BestWifeEver She has coffee, the nurse has Vicodin, this is a good day. I feel like dancing! #BestDayEver

> "Running is like a box of chocolates.
> You never know what you're gonna get."
> — *Forrest's Momma*

Recovery was much quicker than expected. The next couple of days following surgery were bed rest, ice and Motrin. I didn't need the Vicodin. Yes, I kept it and did not flush it down the toilet. I was fearful of the dead goldfish coming back to life under the influence! That was followed by a few days of painful but possible walking, sometimes with crutches. I started commuting to work again. It was a little tough to drive, but I practiced using the crutches to run the pedals in the driveway before venturing out. Then there was physical therapy three times a week, and eventually mile-long walks. The pain slowly subsided, and my upper-body cardio work-outs at the YMCA helped the four weeks pass until I saw the surgeon again.

John, the physical therapist was old-school. He was convinced that running at best would only be a treat. A few miles, a few times a week would probably be it. You need to find something else to do, like swimming or the recumbent bike. Even my runner/podiatrist wasn't so sure that very much running was in my future. "Running would be a treat", those words rang out in my head. And as far as swimming, I had trouble breathing on dry land and kept thinking about undead goldfish in the pool.

I kept walking, doing upper-body cardio at the gym, tuning out the mantras of the physical therapist, following doctors' instructions and praying that I could run again. My four-week follow-up finally came. "How are you today?" asked the doctor.

"I am fine, how are you? Now what about running?" I asked.

He smiled, "Let's see how everything looks first."

He did an exam, bending my knee every which way, twisting, prodding and poking. It really felt good, but of course it was a little weak.

"Now, what about running?" I asked.

"You need to start out slowly. Let's try 20% of what you were doing before the injury." The math turned out to be one mile, two times a week. That's like having a huge box of your favorite chocolates, and only being able to eat two pieces. I was grateful that I would run again, though.

I had been to the podiatrist who made sure I had properly-fitted running shoes, and of course, I vowed to keep doing my leg strength exercises that the physical therapist gave me. I went home and laced up my running shoes. My first run was slow and easy. I walked a half-mile, stretched up against a telephone pole and started down a road with a slight downhill. I ran a few tenths of a mile and then walked some. I had a little pain. With my newly repaired knee, I was a run virgin again - the first time wasn't so romantic, but it was oh so very special.

The next few runs felt pretty good, just a little bit of pain. I kept my word, and stuck to one mile two times a week, and continued in physical therapy. "Running is just a treat," John kept telling me. I kept running twice a week, and went for my two-month check up.

Finally, I heard what I was hoping to hear. "Everything seems just fine, David. Just build up gradually, and stop if you have pain." It was like an alcoholic winning a year's supply of vodka! I went home and ran eight-tenths of a mile (1.2K). It was my longest run without walking since the mile loops on the track when I was in high school. I had some pain, but nothing like before. Two days later I did it again: walk, stretch, run, walk, stretch. It felt good! I decided that for the anniversary of my stay at "Casa del I.C.U.", I would run, walk or crawl a 5K race. I chose the one that was closest to my April fourth anniversary, and registered. I officially started back using the Couch To 5K (C25K) training program so that graduation would be on race day! In my "In It to Lose It" classes, I chided everyone week after week until three of them also registered for the race just to shut me up.

Progress Without Perfection

I admit it, cardio is dangerous, but you still have to try it at home! For lots of beginners, injury from exercising is a real threat which should be addressed. If I had only known what I am about to tell you before it happened to me! I had already had two surgeries since I started this journey, and damn it, neither of them was liposuction! I am not talking about breaking a nail while brushing your hair or having a sore elbow from sitting at the bar doing twelve ounce curls. I am the king of collecting stupid overuse injuries – the kind that stink.

So what do I know that I should share with you? Lots! Before you skip ahead because you just walk, or haven't had any problems thus far, you might want to read on. The older we get, the more likely we are to become injured. I mean you don't see any teenagers rolling on the floor in a television commercial on the phone with 9-1-1 (emergency services) saying, "I've fallen and I can't get up".

I have found that there are a lot of people who want to complete C25K, run a race such as a 5K or 10K or even a half marathon or longer. Others want to do a warrior dash or just walk fast - at least as fast as the dog on the leash! And the rest want ripped abs! You know who you are!

I was tired of being fat and out of shape. I also have a pre-teen that doesn't sit still for a minute. The truth be told, there is little else I would rather do than run. I also swim when I can (where it is not too deep and they have three lifeguards and a defibrillator nearby), ride a bicycle, rollerblade, race around town on an eight-hundred pound motorcycle, play catch, kick the soccer ball, and get out on the ice to skate and play hockey. It's nice to come home from an outing without needing Motrin and an ice pack. Avoiding injuries is actually easy if you follow these steps.

First of all, proper equipment is essential. If you run, get a running store to fit your shoes! Don't just pick up a pair at your local discount store that happens to be your size. If you bike, get the shop to choose a frame height and set up the saddle angle and distance to the pedal so that it fits you. Your joints and tendons will love you for it! Bikers, be sure to get riding shorts, and for the men, they have special seats. Your rear end will love you too. Runners, I suggest tech t-shirts so you don't grind off your nipples. I understand Vaseline and/or Hello Kitty Band-Aids work too. Compression shorts are also important, so that you don't catch your crotch on fire.

If you pole-dance, make sure it's attached to the ceiling and you have properly fitting, er, "gear".

Warm up is also important. Just like your vehicle on a cold morning, you just need to go easy for a few minutes. This supplies blood and oxygen to the body, which helps loosen it up. One of the things I love about running is flying out the door and heading down the street. The change I had to make was a half-mile walk before I run, and a cool down on the way home.

Stretching comes in seven varieties according to the M.I.T. website: ballistic stretching, dynamic stretching, active stretching, passive (or relaxed) stretching, static stretching, isometric stretching, and P.N.F. stretching. Most runners that I know employ some sort of blend. Usually it's dynamic stretching before an exercise as part of the warm up, and ending your routine with static stretching. One of the fastest ways to pull a muscle or tear something is to avoid stretching, or stretch cold muscles. I happen to think yoga is a little too girly, myself. However, it's good for all the things that help you move. I now stretch before I run. I hate the time it takes, but it's worth it. I do it again when I am done. Stretching is essential and, admittedly, sometimes erotic. If you have ever had physical therapy, you know that stretches and strengthening exercises are part of every recovery plan.

Strength helps avoid all sorts of injuries by giving more control to the muscles that manage movement in your joints. If you are going to increase your activity level, you need some basic strength. Even after months of running a hundred miles per month, I discovered my calves were still weak. Because they control foot stability (strike), and when you are tried from racing, it's a recipe for an injury. I had had a couple of them. A regular routine of calf lifts, calf raises, squats, lunges, leg lifts, and high knees keeps the muscles I need for running strong. I have added pushups and planks to get a more rounded workout. All of this is done at home where no one is looking — 'cus, frankly, it ain't pretty.

Cross-Training is good for so many sports. Runners should bike and bikers should swim, and swimmers should run. Mixing up your activity takes the pressure off of certain muscle groups, while building the muscular strength and flexibility you need to maintain your aerobic fitness.

Joints are essential for movement, and your joints need to be cared for. For those that are over fifty, you know there is a big difference from when you were thirty-one. Even those that are younger can enjoy years of injury-free cardio by mixing it up, taking rest days, and staying hydrated. I also use joint supplements, and for me they work really well.

Rest - it is part of every good training program. Even if you are healthy, the proper amount of rest is important. Rest days and time off from the running schedule always show up in faster race times! Sleep is not as overrated as the coffee culture has come to believe.

Overuse injuries can set you back weeks, if not months. As a conqueror, I always tend to overdo things. I did it with running, riding and weight lifting. The key is to start slow and increase as long as you do not have sharp or lingering pain. Muscle soreness and dull aching pains are normal when you push your body to do more than it is used to. The problem with pain is that sometimes it is too late. Although most runners recommend increasing run distances by 10% per week, this may in fact be too fast for you. The same is true for adding weights too quickly on exercise machines or squat racks. It could easily cause a joint or muscle injury. Running on a steep treadmill can cause foot issues too. It's better to take eight weeks to improve, then get hurt the second week and sit out six while you recover.

If you are injured, please see a doctor. Don't just follow instructions in an online thread! Even if it makes some folks think that I'm a nut job, I also believe in the power of prayer; get prayer. I suffered with plantar fasciitis for nearly ten years. I had all the standard treatments from injections to night splints and shoe inserts to ultrasound. I had little or no relief. Finally the fourth podiatrist recommended a new and non-traditional procedure called Platelet Replacement Therapy with Platelet Rich Plasma (P.R.P.). It was very expensive so instead, I went to church one Sunday and decided to ask a couple of friends to pray for my condition. Bob and Walter asked God to heal my foot. It felt a little warm at the time. I was encouraged, and since that time I have had only a little stiffness, but never the kind of pain that would make it hard to get out of bed and make it to the bathroom.

In the midst of my training, I got a little excited and decided to run, and see how fast I could go. I was flying along at twelve miles per hour (marathon pace for a Kenyan!), and pulled something in my hip. I thought I would take a few days off and everything would be great. I was wrong. Whatever the muscle that runs up the inside of the hip joint is called, it hurt. It wasn't bad enough to keep me from running altogether, but still, it hurt. I Googled up some bad news – it ended with "requires surgery" (that seems to come up online a lot - or maybe it's just me). I thought back to how I had handled the knee injury. I'll take it easy for two weeks, and then I am going to see the orthopedic surgeon.

As it turned out, there was a conference on faith healing at my church with two young guys named Josh and Ahab. I was sitting in the back row just enjoying their ministry when Josh said, "there is someone here with hip pain. It's on the inside of the hip. I believe

God wants to heal that now. Who is that?" He then pointed to the section where I was sitting. "Raise your hand." I have had enough experience with supernatural healing to take advantage of it when it comes my way. I stood up and raised my hand. "Well, do something you couldn't do before," he said. I rotated to the left and then to the right. I stood on one foot, placing all my weight on the leg with the injured hip and bent to the left, and then to my right. It was gone. Just gone! "How do you feel?" Josh asked me.

Cautiously I said, "It feels better – a lot better." I was reserving the right for this to be some sort of psychosomatic mumbo-jumbo. When I got home I laced up and went for a two mile run. It was in fact, completely gone.

My toolbox of prevention and injury recovery includes more than prayer (which is always my first choice now). I use every avenue of wellness I can to keep me striding down the road. I have used a chiropractor who believed that staying off an injury is not always the best thing for recovery. He's an Active Release Technique practitioner. I have also had injuries that required RICE: Rest, Ice, Compression and Elevation along with anti-inflammatories. Other injuries responded to ultrasound, while others responded to electric stimulation. Deep tissue massage was helpful for other injuries. There is no magic, universal formula for managing injuries, just listen to your body (as long as it is not telling you to quit, or go on a pizza binge)!

The good news is, that by following my suggestions, you can probably avoid injury altogether and not need doctors, faith healers, ice packs and Motrin.

CHAPTER EIGHT

Run With Heart

I prayed to God to let me run a 5K. Certainly I didn't believe I could run a marathon at the time. It took an entire year to reach my goal, but I eventually made it. Looking back today, as my friend Bobby often reminds me, my can'ts were too big. I also realized that my dreams were too small (or maybe I just needed a little bit bigger faith, knowing that I wouldn't be doing it alone).

The "Run With Heart 5k", My First

The predawn glimmer of morning peeked around the window shades, as the clock silently proclaimed that it was 5:47 AM — it's race day! The slowly-churning thoughts begin their own race in my mind. "Is it raining today?" "Did I remember my favorite headphones?" "Which pair of shoes?" "Am I going to run too fast in the beginning and have to walk in the end?" "Will I look like a dork?" "Oh God, should I really be doing this?"

A little nervous (you think?), I got out of bed, pulled on a t-shirt, headed to the bathroom and eventually made my way to the coffeemaker downstairs. "I am going to finish in thirty minutes or less, and not walk a single step" I told myself, as the smell of freshly-brewing coffee reminded me to get the milk from the refrigerator.

I took a cup of coffee up to my wife and switched on the local news for a weather report. "A fifty percent chance of light showers in Metrowest" announced the happier-than-he-should-be weather-man. I pulled up weather.com for Clinton, Massachusetts on my Android, hoping to get a better deal for the day.

"What if my feet are soaked?" "I am running this race no matter what!" I reassured myself. Silently, I dreaded the possibility of running in the pouring rain. Turning the knobs on the shower faucet and adjusting the temperature, I stepped in. While I was there I prayed for no rain, for the ability to finish, and I thanked God for my amazing health. Give or take a few days, it had been one year since I had been in the hospital.

I switched on the NHL channel as they recapped some of the week's games. I didn't really listen as I laid out my red running outfit: a plain red cotton t-shirt, red basketball shorts, and red pin-striped sweat pants. I clicked off all the other things I would need. Headphones, arm-holder for my smartphone; pretty sure I had everything.

Driving to the race, I kept an eye on the sky and the car's temperature gauge. I don't really remember what was on the radio.

12:15 — I left my wife and daughter in the school parking lot and went to the sign-in table. They found my name and handed me a welcome bag with hearts. I didn't check to see what was inside, I just dropped it off with my wife. I also received my name tag and a "Run with Heart 5K" t-shirt. I headed for the ~~bathroom~~ porta-potty.

12:30 — The parking lot began to fill up with runners and walkers. There were kids, teenagers, young adults and lots of soccer moms with blond ponytails pulled through the back of their baseball caps. Everywhere you looked there was red. Through the crowd, I spotted my eldest daughter as she drove in.

12:35 — My friends from the Monday-Wednesday cardio class appeared from the sea of red. After introducing them to my wife and kids, we posed for an Orange Team photo and made some small talk.

12:50 — Starting my training app and selecting the settings for the race, I checked my play-list, and slipped my smartphone into the arm-holder, attached the headphone cord, and put them on as I adjusted the volume.

12:55 — My friends and I did warm-ups and stretched. I kissed my family and headed for the starting line.

1:00 — The race promoter was on the bullhorn, and I pulled out one of my headphones to hear the announcement. It seemed like forever as we jogged in place to stay warm. I could see my family on the sidelines. I wondered what time it was, trying to focus on racing! Finally a police cruiser pulled up and blipped the siren, signaling the start of the race. The pack began to move ahead, but slowly. I was surrounded by my friends as we worked our way down the first stretch. The Bob Brown Band thumped out the chorus of Tom Petty's "Breakdown". Two of my teammates were in front of me, while two others were beside me. We turned the first corner. "Four-tenths of a mile, speed 6.6 miles per hour," Noom informed me in the headphones.

I was on pace.

Down an easy hill and across the railroad tracks, one of my teammates pulled quickly ahead. Two others were slowly pulling away as well. In my earbuds, Lenny Kravitz broke into a guitar solo as I headed up the first hill. "Speed 5.8 miles per hour", crackled an electronic voice over the soaring guitar. Debating on whether or not to speed up a little to make up some time, I decided to keep my pace. Lengthening my stride a bit as I made my way along the lake, passing the one-mile marker. I waved to the race marshal holding the sign. On the other side of the lake I could see the leaders of the pack off in the distance.

Steppenwolf served up the 60's hit "Magic Carpet Ride" as I sailed into the next mile. So far the weather has held, it was chilly, but as that great statesman Marty Feldman once observed, "it could be worse, it could be raining!"

It was just about then, that it started to drizzle, making it hard to see very far ahead. "Speed 6.2 miles per hour", the voice reported. Despite the rain and going a bit faster — I pressed on. I was starting to feel the fatigue and began thinking that I might need to walk for a bit, but for the time being, I just tried to breathe more deeply and get a little more oxygen. I passed a walker dressed in white, and started up another hill. At the crest, I could see down the road to the two-mile mark and the water station. Tim Hughes' "Happy Day" came on and inspired me to pick up the pace again. I thanked God out loud for his presence.

March 28, 2012

I did it, I ran my first ever 5K! It was a personal record for both time and distance. I believed that I had beaten my heart disease.

The walker in white ran past me.

I shed a few tears; this is why I was here, to celebrate my recovery.

I slowed enough to grab a plastic cup off of the water table and tried to take sip without stopping. I nearly gagged. I coughed a few times and gave up the attempt, then got back on my racing pace again and my digital trainer squawked to me, "Speed 6.2 miles per hour." Had it been a summer race, I'd might have dumped the cup of water on my head to cool me off, but I was already cold and wet so, really, what would have been the point. I just tossed it aside.

I cruised along to "Gypsy Jam", one of my own Hendrix-like instrumental originals. I knew I could cover an entire mile while I blasted out some of my best ever guitar work. Around the bend and in front of me, was an eight percent uphill grade on the other side of the river. I labored to put one foot in front of the other. "Speed 3.8 miles per hour." That is almost walking speed, I thought to myself. I pushed myself until I could see the top of the hill.

I turned right, heading toward town, and saw a couple of runners up ahead. I passed the walker in white again as Joe Satriani began to play in my ears. It was time for the final push to the finish line. "Speed 7.2 miles per hour." I wasn't sure that I could keep up that speed, but I just kept pace with the music as I had done over a hundred times before. Nothing like some fiery licks to coax just a bit more adrenaline from wherever those reserves might be stored.

"Use the auxiliary power, Scotty!"

I rounded the curve, and there, in the foggy distance, the neon orange cones stood silent sentry to the finish line. The red numerals of the time clock showed 30:31. I cranked up the pace ignoring the music. "Speed 9.7 miles per hour." I saw my 8-year-old on the sidewalk, and behind her, my wife and older daughter. I slapped Charlotte a high-five as my wife ran the video and Zöe clapped. 31:22! I got my placement tag and walked back to greet them.

I did it. I had finished the race that I had asked God to let me run.

I didn't walk.

The "Framingham PanCan 5k", Running for a Cause

The week leading up to my third sanctioned 5K was a tough one. It included a friendly game of amateur league hockey. Even though it's a "no hit" league, Wednesday night hockey is a little rough. After scoring a couple of goals, apparently I was deemed a threat to be reckoned with by The Chiefs! One of their much younger defenseman decided to do something about that, and crosschecked me in front of his net, breaking a rib, my ring finger and popping my shoulder out.

Ouch!

Because you can't fix these injuries, I didn't even bother going to the emergency room to have them looked at (yeah, it's a guy thing). I taped my finger using real medical adhesive tape because the duct tape was out back with the Zamboni, managed the pain of the ribs with a few Motrin and twisted my shoulder until it was comfortable enough to drive home from the rink. But, of course, I finished the game!

Saturday morning I showed up at the Framingham PanCan 5K, also known as the Police Chase. A fitness community buddy Stephan and I were on different courses, in different states, however we ran 5Ks at the exact same time. It was his first — you know, he was a race virgin before that! I thought of him as I waited for my pals from the YMCA to show up.

Before you get the impression that I am sort of a running action hero figure, I want to make it clear that I had never run a 5K in my teens, my twenties or my thirties, not even in my forties. I was a 5K virgin until my fifties! For all of my life, up until I was sick, I had a whole list of other things that seemed more important than my health. I smoked as many as three packs of cigarettes a day for twenty years, and ate whatever I wanted. It took me a year to graduate from the twelve-week C25K program! As you already know, that heart attack really got my attention, and I got on the get-healthy-or-die-trying train.

Of course my first race, an American Heart Association run, was awesome because I simply finished, and that really was my goal. The second, a memorial to the fallen hero Officer Savage, was great because I finished in well under thirty minutes, another goal attained. I also liked the race shirts with the police logo silk-screened on the front, and the word "Savage" on the sleeve. What is it about the third one that makes it more special than the others? I ran it in memory of my mother who died of pancreatic cancer on September fourteenth, 2001. It's an awful disease, and I hate it. The race proceeds benefited Pancreatic Cancer Action Network (www.pancan.org).

It was the race that I had been training for. I knew that Mom couldn't actually see me run for her that day, but I felt her presence, especially in those stretches of the race where you just get into the groove, and have time to be alone with your thoughts. It was going to be my best time ever — a personal record.

My little team from the YMCA showed up on a gorgeous sunny morning. We did a short warm up, took our customary team photo, did some stretching together, and jogged around near the starting line until the race was about to get under way. I got a lot of thumbs up for my "Cancer Sucks" t-shirt!

The adrenalin rush on race day is always welcome, and that morning I needed it more than ever! Those ribs were pretty sore (remember the ribs? And the busted finger? And the dislocated shoulder?). If I had known how bad it was, I might not have run;

clearly, ignorance is bliss (another guy thing, I guess). I had read a horrifying story about a woman who had heart failure because she had pre-medicated using Motrin before a race. I decided not to. Besides, I cranked out two miles the day before in record time. I was feeling good…well, good enough anyway. Besides, the distractions of my friends around me and the excitement of anticipation before the race kept me from dwelling on my sorry condition.

The gun went off, and over two hundred runners darted across the starting line. Cruising along to Lenny Kravitz, I had a good pace going a few hundred yards after crossing the timing mats. I thought of how my mom would have enjoyed this beautiful day, as I ran on the brick walk beneath the majestic maples. I passed a large group of runners looking for some space to get back on the mark.

Photo by: Unknown Runner

As I rounded the first corner and pushed on up a short hill, those ribs started to hurt. I tried to ignore the pain. The most annoying thing about bruised ribs is that they hurt more with deeper breaths. I thought quickly that I only had to run about fifteen more minutes, and I could easily do that.

As the pack started to spread out, we crossed the dam at the Framingham Reservoir Number One. The sound of the falls, the fresh cut suburban grass, and the smell of lilacs was in the air; the water glistened in the midday sun. With all of my senses aroused by the sight, the aroma and the sound surrounding me, I couldn't help but think again about my mother, a pastoral scene she would have loved.

But the race commanded my reality at the moment, and that stabbing pain in my side was growing. Up ahead was the mile-one water stop; I don't hydrate (nerd terminology for drinking water) while I am running, but a quick refreshing mouthful was tempting. I slowed enough to grab a cup from one of the volunteers. Drinking and running never goes well for me; bouncing up and down with each foot-fall and, of course, water likes to seek its own level (learned that in science class in junior high school). Bottom line, the water doesn't like to stay put in a paper cup that is being jolted up and down while trying to hit the moving target of my mouth. Did I say that coughing (gagging) and bruised ribs are not friends? Nope — not at all.

I could see my teammate, Cherilynn, up ahead a few hundred yards. She is often the pace-setter of our group from the "Y", and we are always close in time, each of us trying to notch a win over the other. I started thinking that this race would be number three in a best of three series, and I was falling behind. I really didn't want to be beaten by her!

I picked up my pace on a level section of the course, but the pounding of my steps became too intense and my breathing was off. With about half a mile left, I just got in as comfortable a groove as possible, wishing it was all over.

Then it occurred to me that my mother hadn't given up when she was in pain. She did everything that she could do to keep her life as close to normal as possible during her chemo treatments and the final days of her rapidly declining health. We had even spoken on the phone the day she died.

Inspired, I pressed on with renewed determination.

In fact, I sprinted the last 400 yards as fast as I could go. I passed more than a dozen runners as I blasted across the finish line at 11.7 mile per hour.

Because the race was a tad longer than 5K, my time was 29:20. I had lost two out of three to Cherilynn. It wasn't my best time, but it was by far my best effort. I did it for my mom. I did it for those that can't run, and I did it in memory of those whose lives have been robbed by cancer.

It was okay that I had been beaten by a girl.

Then, I went home and took a hot shower, and rewarded myself with x-rays at the emergency room. In the waiting room, I just got the sense that Mom would have been proud of me, maybe not so much for running in a foot race, but for not giving in to the pain, and not giving up when it seemed just to unbearable to continue. Yeah, I'm sure she was smiling about then.

Running Down a Dream

I was just six weeks away from celebrating my first anniversary as a runner — well, after I finally finished C25K the previous March. That day I had my longest run to date. When I started running, I just wanted to finish a 5K and run a few races throughout the year. "Ha!" said the fitness addict, "I have not begun to run!"

It was not my usual long-run day, but because of an impending blizzard, I decided to go for it (who knew how many days we'd be snowed in). I had my first half marathon in just a few weeks, so I needed the workout. The previous day, instead of my regular day at the gym with some cardio and weights, I just went for a two mile walk; that's a rest day for me. But I got up that morning, and the weather report said mostly sunny, and that's my kind of weather. It was 17 degrees Fahrenheit (-8C), so I drank a few mugs of hot coffee and four cups of water while I waited for it to get to at least twenty degrees out. Oh yeah, and I needed a meaningful pilgrimage to the bathroom before I'd venture out into the cold.

At 10:00 AM, I put on all my long-run, low-temp-tested gear. That would be my thicker running socks, my orgasmic Under Armor underwear, a pair of REI running tights which my wife says are for girls (only the pink ones, Dear), sports shorts, two long sleeve UA running shirts, one of which was a turtleneck. Then I added a headband and a pair of thin running gloves. The last time out, I stopped wearing the gloves after eight miles. I didn't really map out a training route, but I know my mileage around town from lots of shorter runs. After 1,200 miles in the same neighborhood, some things are just automatic.

I hate to stretch, so I usually do that in the shower, however, I didn't get one that morning. So off I went with my Bart Simpson hair style, and started a fast walk up around the block past the ice-covered pond. After about four minutes, I pulled up to a telephone pole and stretched things out as the chilly wind blew. Endomondo paused recording. It might have thought I'd frozen to death or something since I'd stopped moving for a few minutes. Then thinking about the two hours ahead of me, I started jogging. It seemed impossible in that cold. Thinking to myself, I wondered if I would have another injury even with all the stretching and exercising I was doing? I prayed not. Off I went, bouncing down the road to a couple of my original guitar tunes. Ten minutes and thirteen seconds later, mile one was behind me.

Up the hill to the state highway, I ran another mile of my 5K course. I split off onto the high school rubberized track to save some wear and tear on my knees. Soon, miles three and four were in the rearview mirror of life. Then I headed out across town, to the park where they have a one-and-a-half-mile paved loop around the 9/11 memorial. Our town lost 19 to that day's tragedy. At mile five, my right foot and knee started to get stiff, so I took a minute to walk and stretch it on a park bench.

No injuries today, please God!

I crossed the Winter Street dam and headed back up the hill to the park where I decided to run it backwards. That means a long steady uphill and a slightly steep downhill. I deserved a little downhill after all the headwinds by the reservoir. Endomondo chirped out the mile six statistics. It was a record 10K: 56:55!

Miles seven, eight and nine passed by as I trudged through the exit gate back towards the house. My legs were starting to feel it, eighty-six minutes in. I began to think I might not make it. I have pushed through the pain and ended up with injuries too many times. I picked up my pace when Israel Houghten came on my headphones singing "Turn it Around".

I ran some more, with the help of Tom Petty's "Running Down a Dream".

I kept running.

After what seemed like a long time, I thought I should have passed ten miles going over the railroad bridge.

I kept running.

Finally I took my Android off of my arm to check. I guess I missed the ten-mile prompt as it was at 10.67 miles. I had to stop to cross the intersection — well, not really. I was dressed in safety green! Sort of my "get the heck out of the way" colors...you'd have to be from Boston (where jay-walking is the second most popular sport next to honking the horn).

I made my way down Franklin Street and ran the "Framingham Turkey Trot" route in reverse. Endomondo clicked off eleven miles. If I headed home then, I wouldn't complete the required twelve miles. I gloried in the fact that I had never run this far before. It was then that I realized I needed to adjust my course to get in all twelve miles, so that I'd land on my door step at the end. My only option was a huge freakin' hill that is 195 feet to the top. My pace slowed to three miles per hour. I started to walk. At the top, rounding the corner I headed down the long slow hill towards my house, made a right on my street, and it happened. My first ever twelve-miler was in the books!

I did my cool-down, walked home, stretched on the front porch and went inside to get warmed up and do my happy-dance with a fresh cup of hot coffee.

CHAPTER NINE

Why I Hate Running

Back when my treadmill walks turned into runs, I decided to risk the elements and went outside where the wild things are. I braved the heat of summer, the frigid cold of winter, the snow, loose dogs, and the insanity of Metro Boston traffic. Some drivers don't have a clue, others just drive with blinders on, and still others are a mixture of both. After what I said to a couple of drivers that particular morning, I was praying that St. Peter had a soft spot in his heart for runners.

How did I go from blissful sleep and dreams of conquering a loaf of bacon for breakfast to dodging maniacal Bentown drivers? I was a little late getting started that day because shoulder pain from my rotator cuff surgery had kept me up for a few hours during the night. I usually have a cup of coffee about 5:00 while I read my email and comment on my friends' accomplishments in the news feed of the fitness community I belong to by copying and pasting "WTG" (way to go!) on their postings. I am not really a morning person and, without coffee, I probably would copy and paste "WTF" (who's the fool!) and not even know it. I managed to get one cup in between 6:30 and 7:00, but that is just not enough! The lack of caffeine can ruin a whole freakin' morning in a matter of minutes! It's one of the reasons I hate running. You have to go early and feign lucidity and alertness without hurting yourself or others.

It was my five mile training run day, which wasn't off to a very good start. I enjoyed a few minutes of the news and then a pile of political ads came on, so I got dressed to run. I feel sort of weird being naked in front of my wife and then walking out the door for a run, but a man has to do what a man has to do (as long as I remember to get dressed *before* I walk out the door). Besides, she called my Nike Combat running underwear ~~gay~~ effeminate.

I kissed her goodbye — I mean you never know if I will come home (we're talking Boston traffic, remember) — and then fiddled with my running app on the way downstairs to get my headphones and smartphone arm holder. "Arm holder" sounds like my arm disconnects and needs some support, but "arm band" sounds like I am a terrorist — but I digress. I made a pit stop before heading out the door; it was then that I noticed trouble on the horizon. What happens in the bathroom before a run directly affects your run. Runners have a variety of terms for fecal success such as, "lift off", "log jam", "hit the jackpot", and my favorite, "completed the election count."

I opened the front door and got a blast of the cool, crisp fall air that gave my nipples an appreciation for their female counterparts. I hate the cold, too, I thought.

I try not to run in the same routes each day. It's a well known fact that sexual predators stalk runners to become familiar with their route in order to plan a future attack, and an action hero like me has to be careful of such things (not). The real reason that I change it up is because otherwise, quite frankly, it's boring — although I do have two lakes in the neighborhood which are always quite beautiful, and you never know when I might spy a mermaid or Nessie or something on one of my runs, so I always include them in any route. In order to train for my first half marathon, I had mapped a bunch of routes in my neighborhood in varying distances from three to thirteen miles. Caffeine-deprivation caused me to forget how the heck to start my 5-miler, though. As I was bouncing down the sidewalk to warm up, I just decided to run and listen to my GPS in the headphones.

I did a short, brisk walk (not the walking-the-dog walk) and some stretching on the sidewalk using a handy telephone pole which, always seems to garner the attention of sexual predators and old ladies that want to ask if I am alright.

"You look a little pale, sir," by her expression, I knew she was thinking that the problem with this world is there are too many freaks, not enough circuses.

"No need to call 9-1-1, it's just because I am freezing my nipples off, but thank you for your concern." I replied with a fake smile. "I hate nosy people." I muttered under my breath, as it turned to a visible waft of condensation.

With my tunes in gear, I started down the sidewalk to the likes of Tom Petty and the Heartbreakers. It was then I noticed my right shoe was loose, so I stopped to tie it. Back on pace, I headed up the hill towards the lake in time to see the sea mist clearing in the dawn's early light and the rockets' red glare.

Outside, in the cold distance (thanks Bob and Jimi), my shin started with this weird pain. I decided to make a mental inventory of all my joints to see how things were going. I turned out that there were too many impulse generating points of synaptic displeasure to count, so I decided to focus on the music. Ah yes, "Magic Carpet Ride", it gave me flashbacks to the 70s which I really don't remember (thanks Corey); therefore I cannot validate their validity as a viable reality.

Back in the real world, I noticed my running shorts started falling down. Apparently due to the toxic low levels of caffeine, I guess I didn't tie them after my little trip to the voting booth. To save precious seconds, I decided to re-tie them while running at eight miles per hour. It was sort of like Dale Earnhardt Jr. texting during the Daytona 500. Tightening the knot, I caught a single body hair which caused simultaneous neural impulses, sucking all available electrical current to the neediest receptor in my entire body. This in turn signaled an "I won the lottery" type scream reaction! Dogs barked, mothers rushed their children in from the street, grown men grabbed revolvers from the nightstand, and woman submitted me for the "Neighbor from Hell" episode of Dr. Phil.

Embarrassed, I tore around the corner before their smartphone cameras could record the moment (really didn't relish seeing a rerun of it all on YouTube). Finally, I started to settle into a comfortable pace and got back to my music. I took out my air-guitar, and Bruce and I did a duet during the chorus of "Born to Run". Unfortunately it was trash day in the neighborhood, and for the next mile I cursed Mr. Rogers as the sidewalk had become an obstacle course. In the midst of dodging stinky garbage cans piles of plastic Hefty garbage bags, forcing me onto a lawn, I stepped on a stick which fought back by puncturing my right calf. What next, I thought?

My new route took me by a school where I met a very nice crossing guard. Holding a cup of hot coffee in one hand and her other thumb you know where, she didn't seem too interested in doing much of anything to help me cross the street. I stepped into the crosswalk without her assistance because I am big boy who looks both ways. Just as I took a step, a school bus ran the stop light and cut me off. I let out a string of expletives, which seemed to get everyone's attention! Through the back window of the bus, a Kindergartner gave me thumbs up.

I muttered, "forgive them Father, they just don't know how stupid they are", and headed down the road.

With about a mile or so to go, I just wanted to get home and log my efforts because I knew my family and friends would think I was awesome for not dying. If they had been with me on that particular run, they'd have appreciated just what a feat that really was.

I hate running, I thought.

I trudged on. I ran down by the pond to give the finger to the hospital where I was in the I.C.U. and shouted "I am never going back!" Close to home, I began to think about how inviting the bathroom was going to be when I got in the door – I never had lift off. Thinking about it, I decided to change my weigh in day to that very day.

As I slowed to a walk a block from my house to cool down, it was there the endorphins starting talking to me. And that's why I *love* running!

Whodunit, the Mystery of the Garbage Bag Bandit

Nearly every run I have ever taken started from my front steps. Living in the largest town in the United States has its rewards. We have great facilities including an ice rink, a new football complex with a track and tennis courts, walking trails, parks, an art museum, internationally-known companies, a variety of educational options, a state university, and crime.

After completing morning vespers replete with two mugs of coffee, answering emails, wisecracking on Facebook posts, and a short-but-successful trip to the resort island of *el baño,* I pulled on my running gear and ran though my pre-flight checklist. (It's interesting; there was a time when I didn't have a checklist. I left the house in my compression underwear and no shorts. My neighbor was horrified.) Shoes, socks, underwear, shorts, tech-t, smartphone, door key, ID, arm wrap (proper name for the thingy that holds your phone on your arm), and headphones.

I double-checked my laces. Standing up, I made sure I had the door key and then pulled the headphones over my ears. I plugged the mini-jack into the phone as I walked across the dining room towards the porch door. Stepping out onto the farmer's porch, it was time to start Endomondo and queue up a playlist. Fully intent on the songs needed for my run, I walked across the tiny front yard, sidestepping one of our hundred-year-old maple trees; which was not always my custom. Just as I set foot on the pavement of our tiny street with five houses, I heard the squealing of tires. I kept scanning my playlist to make sure it had my favorite songs in the correct order so that my run would have negative splits. There were more screeching tires, slamming doors — I stepped back onto the sidewalk. I ignored the shouting until it became so loud I finally looked up. There in front of me was an armed policeman with his gun pointed in my direction, "get back in the house!" he yelled.

"Huh?"

"GET BACK IN THE HOUSE!" he screamed at me. I turned around to see nine police cars had crowed the street in front of my home. They had guns drawn and were shouting for someone in my neighbor's yard to "get on the ground!" I walked back across my lawn to the house. I thought, "I can't run without music."

I watched the rest of the scene unfold before me, from the window of the dining room. As the gravity of what was happening set in, I decide to visit the voting booth and check the ballot box one more time.

Not long after, the police have their man in custody. He was covered from head to toe in black garbage bags. This is a criminal? Seriously? Hasn't he seen "Herbie Goes to Monte Carlo"? What kind of crook dresses up in garbage bags? Eventually he was carted away, and there was just one cop left chatting on a cell phone leaning against the front fender of his cruiser. Out the door I went and walked over to him and waited until he finished his call. "What was all that about?" I inquired.

"Just some two-bit-slug breaking into local businesses," he said.

"Wow – well, glad you caught him."

"Oh yeah, catching him was easy, he broke into the donut shop while it was open," he smiled with pride. Sometimes the crooks make the cops' jobs easier by exercising their Constitutional right to being stupid.

"Thanks," I replied as I turned to start my run. When I returned home, I found the story of the "Garbage Bag Bandit" online. I shook my head as I thought, "we need smarter crooks in this town." But then again, it's probably a good thing that they're as dumb as they are.

A Cloud Far Off

Training for a marathon is not as hard as it sounds, we runners just make it sound like rocket science and basic training on Paris Island to impress folks. But, truthfully, planning the training is like solving Rubik's Cube wearing mittens. Marathon training plans initially require a minimum of four days a week, including a day of cross training. It starts out consuming three hours of your week. As time progresses, the time demand climaxes at about ten hours, within just a few months.

For those that can afford the time commitment of four to six runs a week, there is also the strategic factor in planning your training. You need to work around the weather, family activities, holidays, injuries and doctors' appointments – and the "honey do" and the "honey *don't* do" lists. For me, it was "Tetris", the reality show.

After rearranging my schedule to avoid summer thunderstorms and a couple of *have-to* family engagements, I managed to get in all of my long, slow runs. On one of those days, my most reliable running buddy picked me up at the front of the house, and we headed south to the Blackstone Bike Path for our eighteen-miler. It was overcast with a slight chance of rain, so we lubed up our ~~privates~~ most-likely-to-chafe areas with Body Glide, taped our nipples, tied our shoe laces, hit the restroom at Mickey D's, and set out for our three-hour ~~tour~~ adventure. After an easy two miles, it began to rain — no, check that, it started to freakin' *pour*! Ducking into a donut shop, we asked for a plastic bag to cover our electronics.

With the iPhone, the Garmin, and the Fitbit covered, we looked at each other and, shaking our heads in an acceptance of the inevitable, we decided to go for it. For the first few soggy miles we discussed calling it off and returning to the car. After six miles we considered ending it again, the rain was just not letting up. Our lives were locked into this opportunity — we just kept on running. It rained so hard my bifocals became a many-faceted galaxy of kaleidoscopic and psychedelic *oozes,* turning the road into a river of liquid darkness running through the abyss beneath my feet. For the non-drug users, I could not see my feet in front of me.

I followed Scott as he navigated the bike path; it appeared that we were the only badass runners on this often-crowded venue. For two solid hours it rained; the customary sound of our running shoes going "plod-plod-plod" against the pavement was replaced by "splash-splash-splash" as we continued on in the driving rain. As we crossed an intersection where the bike path was protected by a Jersey barrier, I could see that there was nearly two feet of runoff on other side of it! At one of the joints between two sections, it was leaking badly, flowing through like a small river. "Scott! Stick your finger in the dyke or we are all going to drown!" I yelled over the roar of the heavily-falling rain.

As we entered our third hour on the run, the deluge finally stopped (of course, perfect timing, we were nearly to the end of our course). The sound of our rain-soaked running shoes, gasping for air, and spritzing water from their vent holes could be heard for the next few miles.

Soaking wet, chafed, tired, and armed with a story to share at the next million cocktail parties, we were done. We had faced the elements and emerged unscathed (more-or-less) and victorious (right after a couple hot cups of coffee and showers). Hail the conquering action heroes!

You Know What Frosts My Pumpkin?

Placing pumpkins on the front steps leading up to the front door has been a tradition since I can remember. For the most part, people just look at them from afar, while a few little kids come in for a closer look. Then there are those rotten unsupervised teenagers with nothing better to do (I speak from experience, but then I digress). They seem to think smashing the neighbor's pumpkins is a wise idea. I suppose the odds of successfully sneaking up to the front door under the cover of darkness to mug an unsuspecting and defenseless fruit and get away with it, are pretty high.

We had four dogs at the time, although by the time you read this our application for a kennel license may have been approved, removing that limit. One of them is a witch, according to the most current breed information. She spends her time growling for hours to protect a piece of lint or food discarded by the other three. When she barks, it is because something is wrong. The other ones bark because they can (it's a dog thing). One night she barked at three in the morning, we had someone trying to break in the porch door.

But on the night in question, she barked like she meant it, so I went to take a look. As I peered through the window, there were three boys just about to walk away with my kid's sentimental Magic Marker artwork. I guess it's fortunate that I have a pile of running shoes in my office. Putting some on, I slipped out the side door as they were hurriedly heading down the street with their prize.

Once they figured out I was after them, they dropped my pumpkins and took off running at full speed. The chase was on. I run for a lot of causes, from The American Heart Association to the local Boys and Girls Club — this time — this was personal, this was about honor and family pride, justice, and the American way. I not only wanted to save my pumpkins, but I wanted the pumpkin-nappers caught! I confess that I was one of these little thieves growing up, and I knew what they were thinking. I was also pretty certain they hadn't planned an escape route.

They took an unfortunate route, one with a river on one side and a train track on the other. It was like herding pigs to the slaughter. If I could beat them to the bridge, there would only be one way out. I gave out a little Dracula sort of laugh and kicked it in to high gear. I was quickly gaining on them shouting like the mad man that I am (when dealing with the criminal element when they invade your life, a good policy is to make them believe you're absolutely bat-crazy, then they'll believe you're liable to do anything, then just let their collective imaginations do the rest of the work). And there on the one lane bridge, I caught one by the jacket collar and then grabbed a second one by the sleeve. The third one gave up easily.

The rest is in the police report.

On the way back I was feeling pretty proud of myself, and pictured the headline: FAT OLD GUY CHASES DOWN YOUTHFUL PUMPKIN THIEVES. This is big news in a town like mine. Clearly the people in my town slept more peacefully after that, knowing that the mad runner was living amongst them (maybe I really am an action hero, but my wife still makes me take out the trash and clean the litter box).

CHAPTER TEN

You Really Are What You Eat

By definition, a diet is simply what we eat, not a weight loss program. We all have diets. It is a list of everything we consume that our body metabolizes, for better or for worse. For some of us, it's pizza and beer, and for others it's organic vegetables and water. There is no perfect diet except for the *Whole-Food-Caffeine-Fueled-Carnivore-Sushi-Diet,* which I invented (more about that later, again, for better or for worse). Because there are many factors to our metabolic make-up including genetics, age, activity levels, and consumption of various drugs (including medications, nicotine, caffeine and alcohol), each one of us needs a finely-tailored diet. Certainly there are core requirements that are healthy for all of us; take chocolate for example. Who doesn't benefit from chocolate? Chocolate should be a food group! It has antioxidants, while some studies show it *may also* lower cholesterol, help prevent heart disease, improve your skin, and reduce pain in lab rats. A small percentage of women say that chocolate helps in reducing the effects of PMS. As a male, I have no experiential opinion on that, however I am willing to give it a try.

Before we begin, here is the not-so-fine-print. I am *not* an expert, but I see myself playing one on T.V. in my mind's eye. Which, incidentally, should have been poked out a long time ago. I believe you will find the information below reliable, although it is possible that it completely false, and that eating fast food and sugary treats is actually the diet we were meant to eat since the creation of the world. My personal experience, which includes working with health care professionals, is incomplete, lopsided, biased and therefore only suggested as a starting point to increase the variety of potentially healthy foods in your diet. This information is gleaned from sources too numerous to list. I did acknowledge some of the studies on the "acknowledgements" page which you did not read, of course, because you turned directly to the chapter on sex.

Superfoods

If you *have* to eat, you might as well eat *superfoods*! I am not talking about the kinds of foods that will propel you into a trophy run at the National Farting Championship with your patented two-tone-tuba-flutterbug. Nor am I talking about foods that will allow you to stay on the couch and melt fat like you had a liposuction procedure watching *The History of Sex* on the Discovery Channel. Nope! I am talking about the calorie-sparse and nutrient-rich foods which deliver the healthy nutrients needed to build a strong immune system, lower your cancer risk, decrease blood pressure, care for your heart, prevent your legs from cramping after a run, and keep your insulin within tolerable ranges. Think of these foods like the Swiss Army Knife of the food world. These are foods that can meet most of your daily requirements for high-quality carbohydrates, protein, and healthy fat while providing essential vitamins and macronutrients as well as pleasure for your taste buds.

Almonds - Eating almonds has the same effect as the cholesterol-lowering drugs called statins. They are a source of vitamin E, magnesium, protein, fiber, potassium, calcium, phosphorus and iron. Also, almonds (and other nuts) contain phytochemicals, which are plant chemicals that *may* provide protection against heart disease, stroke, and other chronic diseases.

Apples - Apples are a source of both soluble and insoluble fiber. Soluble fiber such as pectin actually helps to reduce the possibility of heart disease. The insoluble fiber provides bulk in the intestinal tract, holding water to cleanse and move food quickly through the digestive system, thus slowing the absorption of calories! Vitamin C content is just underneath the skin, so eat that too!

Avocados - Avocados provide essential nutrients, including fiber, potassium, Vitamin E, B and folic acid (iron). They also act as a "nutrient booster" by enabling the body to absorb more fat-soluble nutrients such as alpha and beta-carotene and lutein in foods that are eaten with the fruit.

They are fatty, but it's the *good* fat, so enjoy a couple each week, or make some fresh guacamole!

Beans - Fiber and protein are the essential nutrients in beans. I like garbanzo beans (chickpeas), adding them to salads. This one will get you a high rating for breaking wind though, as you propel your way to health! Red beans, such as kidney beans, all provide antioxidants. Be sure to drain and rinse canned beans to get rid of as much of the water-borne sodium as possible.

Blueberries - Rich in Vitamins K and C, which helps in absorption of iron while improving the immune system. They also provide plenty of fiber, enhancing the digestion process. A rich source of manganese, they aid in bone development as well as in the metabolism of fats, proteins, and carbohydrates; and they turn your tongue blue, which is always fun!

Broccoli - Low in carbohydrates, this superfood contains more vitamin C than an orange! And, a serving of broccoli contains as much calcium as a glass of milk! Add to that, iron, vitamin K, fiber and potassium. Rivaled by bananas for potassium content, it is great for body building, and reducing the effects of muscle cramps.

Cinnamon - Possibly on the Voodoo list of herbal remedies, however, studies showed that it reduced the proliferation of leukemia and lymphoma cancer cells. When consumed with honey, it aided in reduction of arthritic pain. One study found that smelling cinnamon boosts cognitive function and memory, and another found that cinnamon fights the E. coli bacteria in unpasteurized juices, as well as lowering blood sugar and cholesterol. Me, I just like it with apples.

Dark Chocolate - It helps lower high blood pressure and contains antioxidants which are good for your immune system. In fact, I find chocolate good for reducing an occasional case of the blues, while I recline with my pink bunny slippers.

Dried Fruit – A concentrated version of their un-dried fruit counterpart, containing most of the same benefits minus the water. They are good for snacks, but be sure to watch the calories!

Extra Virgin Olive Oil - The good fat. Excellent for your joints, full of antioxidants, it's heart-healthy and may prevent oxidation, which causes cell damage, reducing the risk of cell aging and osteoporosis. I am no virgin, but it sounds good to me.

Garlic - *The New York Times* said it best: "The power to boost hydrogen sulfide production may help explain why a garlic-rich diet appears to protect against various cancers, including breast, prostate and colon cancer, say the study authors. Higher hydrogen sulfide might also protect the heart, according to other experts. The concentration of garlic extract used in the latest study was equivalent to an adult eating about two medium-sized cloves per day."

I ate a huge clove with my seafood dinner while I was on a date with my wife. It's a good thing, because when I looked into her eyes, my heart would have stopped without it. But for some reason, she didn't want to kiss me after that.

Honey - Antioxidants, energy boosting, and a lower glycemic index than sugar, it is proposed to have some magical anti-aging properties. Here is my take, if it's good enough for Winnie the Pooh, then it's good enough for me!

Greek Low-Fat or Non-Fat Yogurt - Both Greek and regular yogurt are part of a healthy diet. They are low in calories, packed with calcium and live bacterial cultures. However the Greek variety is strained to remove most of the liquid whey, lactose, and sugar. In roughly the same amount of calories, it doubles the protein and cuts the sugar content in half!

Oats – Loved by horses on every continent, oats, full of fiber, are one of the best whole grains. Studies concluded that consumption of oats (or any whole grains) was linked to a lower risk of death from diseases that are triggered by inflammation, including heart disease and diabetes. Post-menopausal woman may like them too!

Onions - Bad for your breath, but the sulfur (a compound) and quercetin (a flavonoid) are good for you. They are also in the group of fruits and vegetables referred to as negative calorie foods (another mystical claim!), which require more calories to digest than you will get from eating them. Add to that celery, carrots, cucumbers, lettuce and peppers, along with 2 dozen others, and you are likely to lose weight while still eating substantially filling amounts.

Oranges - Get part of your daily dose of soluble fiber and vitamin C. Vitamin C from oranges and other citrus fruits is much more likely to be used by the body than that from supplements.

Soy - It's what tofu is made out of and full of protein. It just happens to be my least favorite thing on this entire list. Soy itself is not the superfood, it is the fermented soy products such as miso, tempeh or soy tofu sauce. To be fair, I will add that there is generally some debate over the healthiness of soy products.

Sweet Potatoes - A starchy vegetable packed full of vitamin A and fiber, and lower in carbohydrates than white potatoes. Just skip the candied yams!

Spinach - Popeye the Sailor was right about spinach. Spinach is a good source of niacin and zinc, as well as a very good source of fiber, protein, vitamins A, C, E (Alpha Tocopherol), K, thiamin, riboflavin, B6, folate, calcium, iron, magnesium, phosphorus, potassium, copper and manganese. This powerhouse food is low in calories and good quality carbohydrates. It is doubtful anyone could eat too much of it! One caveat, vitamin K and blood thinners may be in conflict, so check with your doctor.

Tea (Green, Red or Black) - Drinking green tea reduces the risk of esophageal cancer by nearly sixty percent according one study! It also helps reduce cholesterol. Green tea's antioxidants, called catechins, scavenge for free radicals that can damage DNA and contribute to cancer, blood clots, and atherosclerosis. Red tea is full of antioxidants but contains no caffeine.

Tomatoes - No matter how you like your tomatoes, pureed, raw, or in a sauce, you're eating vital nutrients like vitamin C, vitamin E, and iron. Early research suggests lycopene was helpful in reducing the risk of cardiovascular disease, cancer, diabetes, osteoporosis, and even male infertility. Just be sure to watch the sugar and sodium content of canned and bottled tomato products by reading the label.

Turkey - White meat turkey is lower in calories than any other meat, including chicken. It contains calcium, protein, and it's low in fat and naturally low in sodium!

Walnuts - One ounce of nuts can go a long way in providing key healthy fats while managing hunger. Other benefits are a dose of magnesium and fiber. If you suffer from IBS, I suggest trying a half ounce of cashews twice a day!

Wild Salmon - I have an ounce of salmon 3 or 4 days a week as part of my breakfast sandwich. Experts say that eight or nine ounces are very good for us. Studies have shown that we lose more weight when consuming an equal amount of salmon calories versus beef, chicken, pork or turkey calories.

Food with Benefits - Aphrodisiac Foods

Why wait for the day on which Cupid unloads his quiver of love-drunk arrows upon mankind. Ever since Santa lost weight, he's been moonlighting as the Little Love Archer. The following list of food, "food with benefits", can get him to visit most any day of the year. According to AlterNet.org, there are ten foods that should increase the odds of you getting lucky. I also found a list of ten on the Fitness.com site and six more on Shape.com. Today is as good as any to stop practicing and mate!

Asparagus - I don't know what's in there, but I like 'em. As far as sex goes, I'm not thinking that my wife will appreciate the fiber -- if you know what I mean -- but, apparently they boost the production of histamine, which helps with orgasms. I can't be positive, but maybe if you have a cold it can help cure that too. I think the best thing they have going for them is their shape. Possibly if you had a long enough one you could use it for a whip (but I digress).

Almonds - Now we're talking. I love almonds. If they were liquid, I would take a bath in them. Instead of tequila, I think you can use them for body shots. I guess they were fertility symbols at one time. I am thinking: without nuts, there isn't much chance – just a thought. The article said that it works best on women, which is probably why I don't know.

Avocado - The Aztecs called the avocado ahuacuatl, or "testicle tree." After you stop laughing, think about all the uses the pit might have. I think we are done talking about avocados.

Bananas - The banana is no stranger to sexual activity. I was at a party once...never mind. Apparently, if you eat them, it increases the male libido. I think when I was a teenager it worked. I still eat bananas, but I guess I am immune to their effect nowadays. I'd probably have better luck if someone else would eat it and I watched.

Basil - Now I really like basil in my food. It is common spice in my house. But when it comes to increasing sexual desire, I never thought of keeping a shaker of it in the bedroom. I guess the only drawback is if my wife says, "What's that in your teeth?" Until then, I think we'll stick to Chanel No. 5.

Black Raspberries - Known for enhancing amorous desire because of something in the seeds. They are supposed to increase your endurance. So smear them on all over and party-party!

Broccoli - The Vitamin C apparently increases the female libido. Who would have guessed little green wannabe tree could have such power? I have also seen it hanging from brightly-colored ribbons on front doors during the harvest season. I suppose it is like mistletoe at Christmas. I'll have to check and see if there are any skid marks in front of those houses.

Chocolate - I am with you on this one. I like chocolate so much; I would have sex by myself.

Cloves - There is some magical power which increases the sexual activity of males. I didn't realize males needed any encouragement, except to unplug the cable. It's probably because it reminds them of a holiday ham baked in beer.

Eggs - Of course...eggs! They contain some supernatural amino acid that is used to treat erectile dysfunction.

Figs - Ever since the time of Adam and Eve, there seems to have been some reproductive mystery surrounding figs. My thought is that the first couple was created without children, so no one was banging on the bedroom door asking for a glass of water. On the other hand, figs make me think of camels, and camels make me think of spitting – all of a sudden it's not working.

Garlic - It's good for your heart and your blood flow; it's the Viagra of the natural world! Now guys, if you can get her to get close enough after eating it, you might be in luck. My wife said it would probably be better if I mowed the lawn and took out the garbage instead.

Ginger - Another root with more mystical medicinal attributes than penicillin; it is proposed to be a sexual enhancement remedy. Time alone without kids has a similar effect on males.

Ginseng - According to researchers at the University of Hawaii, this wonder-root improves the female libido when taken over a period of a month. Time alone without kids has a similar effect on females.

Honey - Well, it is supposed to increase hormones, which make us want to rip our mate's clothes off! The problem at my house is that I can't get the stupid cover off it once it has been previously opened, and the desire is gone if I get so frustrated with the petrified jar lid and have to go shopping.

Lettuce - Iceberg lettuce apparently contains an opiate which helps activate the sex drive. Apparently, rabbits have known this for a long time!

Oysters - Some people believe that anything that looks like the flu is suspicious. I think they are missing out. I will admit that this is my favorite food. While I only eat them on rare occasions, I am going to check the calendar to see how lucky they made me!

Saffron - Though it's not exactly champagne and chocolates, it too, is purported to improve sexual functioning. Because it is one of the most expensive spices, I suggest sticking with the booze and chocolate.

Sushi - Sushi contains raw fish. There is nothing sexier than a mate who consumes raw fish in spite of the warnings on the restaurant menu. One evening, my wife and I were on a date at an Asian restaurant, and I put in a little extra wasabi in the soy dipping sauce. It had a bit of a kick (read: fried our eyeballs), and my wife's contact lens cascaded down her cheek into the flaming PuPu platter. Sushi is good, but is not an aphrodisiac.

Watermelon - According some experts, this is the Viagra of the fruit world! And boys, please remember, spitting your seeds (no matter how accurate or far) is not romantic.

I'd be interested to see if putting a little of each into a blender or juicer would make love potion number 10? For now, I have decided to take my chances with flowers, chocolates and a thoughtful card - right after I mow the lawn.

Unhealthy Health Foods

You may have read Dr Seuss' *Red Fish Blue Fish*, but did you ever ask yourself how they got to be that color? What about the green eggs and ham? Not all foods are as healthy as you might think.

I'd bet, as many others, you have fallen prey to food advertising. Food manufacturers spend billions of dollars just to give us the impression that certain foods support *weight loss*, are *heart-healthy*, and are *all natural* or *organic*. The truth is that there are few legal guidelines for what food companies can say about their products. Organic food labeling has some of the strictest guidelines, but even that may not be what you think it is.

What's the key to success in choosing the healthiest foods? You need to read the freakin' label (RTFL)! Having a healthy diet is not all about calories. Ingredients really do matter. I just want to say, I am not a health food or organic fanatic, however; when you get to be my age, some of the wear-and-tear of unhealthy food consumption becomes more apparent. True story.

Here is a list of foods I innocently thought were going to help me lose weight, get healthy, and look like Arnold Schwarzenegger.

Breakfast Cereals - Cereals that are made from whole grains are the best. The truth is even some of those have sugar, salt and chemically-based minerals, and additives. Here are some of the ingredients from a popular *all natural* heart healthy brand cereal: cane syrup, salt, canola oil, [unidentified] natural flavor, and a few other things none of us can pronounce.

I prefer to make my own breakfast sandwich. They are simple to make: One whole wheat mini-bagel, a poached egg, and a piece of salmon with a slice of low-fat Swiss cheese. I switch out the salmon for a slice of tomato and a few leaves of spinach for a Florentine version. You can make a spread with salsa and Greek yogurt too. If you are really lazy like I am, just purchase a breakfast sandwich maker online for about $30!

Yogurt- Which one should you pick? There are so many choices, it's like winning the lottery and choosing a new luxury car. You can narrow the field by choosing Greek yogurt (a superfood). Non-Greek yogurts are just not as healthy (check the sugar content!). Many of the non-fat or low-fat yogurts are loaded with sugar. I am not a fan of artificial sweeteners. Food companies add a minimum of fruit to make you feel good about eating it. Be sure to look at the ingredients on frozen yogurts too!

Have you asked yourself this question: When was key lime pie or cheesecake healthy? When it was yogurt! Right!

Bread - Don't be fooled, the labels m*ulti-grain* and *wheat* on bread packaging do not make it healthy. Refined grains don't hold a candle to whole grains. Dark bread can still contain trans-fats and low quality carbs, which can offer reduced fiber content and keep you from obtaining your weight loss goals.

Sandwiches - It is hard to make a healthy sandwich. Too much bread, even the good stuff is not the best use of your calories. Processed meats and cold cuts like turkey, ham and chicken can contain a day's worth of sodium, along with saturated fats and cholesterol. In addition, high-calorie dressings and toppings add to the potential for a caloric tsunami!

If you are going to have a sandwich, think *half*, and find a soup or suitable nutritious companion. There are some dressings you can use to keep the calories down. Substituting Greek yogurt with a little vinegar can take the place of mayonnaise, mustard is a great option, and hummus or goat cheese make great spreads too. Drop on some spinach instead of lettuce, a little tomato, and a ring or two of onion, and you are ready for lunch.

Fruit Juice - Can you say added sugars? Many, with the exception of pulp-retained juice (which I think has a weird texture), offer a fraction of the value of the real fruit! Remember, water is your friend!

Frozen Diet Meals – There is nothing wrong with frozen fruits and vegetables, unless they have added sugar. It is the dinners from the diet chains, and so-called "lean meals", that often have 400 to 600 mg of sodium or more. They may be easy to prepare, but these 300 to 500 calorie dishes often lack whole grains, and contain processed meat, which has trans-fats and cholesterol. There is a solution, cook and freeze leftovers that you have carefully chosen the ingredients for yourself.

Sports/Energy Drinks – The neon-colored drinks contain large quantities of caffeine, sugar (carbohydrate), and possibly some electrolytes, but not much else. It is best to fuel up for your workouts in advance with some carbs, and replenish your body with protein when you are done. (Some experts say carbs after as well).

If you are a long-distance runner, bicyclist, or swimmer who exercises for an hour or more, there are some other considerations. The main need is hydration, but aerobic efficiency drops over time, and carbohydrates take over fueling the body. The average sports and energy drinks don't always cut it.

Fast Food Salads – High-calorie dressings, many with sugar, croutons made with white flour, and poor quality vegetables topped with fried chicken, equal a diet disaster! You are probably better off ordering a double cheeseburger!

Granola/Protein Bars - Good granola bars consist of healthy oats and sometimes nuts. The problem is what they are held together with. Some of the least healthy ingredients include dried cane syrup, soy extracts, lecithin, salt, and chocolate chips which makes them candy bars.

Cheese - This is another one that can make or break your weight loss, and blow up a good diet. There are some cheeses that are low in fat and low in sodium. Goat cheese is probably the best choice. I can assure you that Cheez-Its are not on the list!

Diet Soda - All sweetened diet foods contain artificial sweeteners such as aspartame. I suggest doing a web search for more information. Water is always your best option, and sparkling water with a twist of citrus or fruit slice can make it a little more interesting. Water with cucumber and a sprig of mint is another more flavorful drink.

Veggie Chips - Many of these potato chip replacements are made of vegetable flour, and don't contain much in the way of real vegetables. Even the better ones can contain cane syrup, sorghum flour, loads of salt, and yes, even sugar!

Supplements – I am *not* a fan of processed supplements regardless of whether they are produced organically or not. Supplements are good if you cannot stay within a reasonable daily caloric intake level and get enough of the essential nutrients to fuel your body. From everything that I have read, it's hard to know exactly what you need, and at what capacity your body is able to use them. According to Roni Caryn Rabin in a *New York Times* blog dated December 16, 2013, "One in two adults takes a daily vitamin pill, and Americans spend tens of billions of dollars each year on supplements."

According to Dr. Poly, a multivitamin with minerals is a smart move because eating perfectly every day isn't very likely to happen, even for a proficient nutritional expert. Lab/blood work and physical assessments will not tell you if you are deficient in a particular vitamin or mineral unless you have a moderate or severe deficiency. In her expert opinion, that is far too late to address any deficiencies. The body works to maintain homeostasis in the blood; therefore, most labs are generally normal even with an ongoing deficiency until the disease process occurs. The clearest example of this axiom is calcium. Your blood will maintain a normal calcium level even with a moderate deficiency. If needed, the body will draw calcium out from the bones to maintain normal blood levels which will lead to osteopenia and osteoporosis. "You want to correct calcium intake far before bone disease occurs," she said.

The good news is, it's hard to overdose on supplements. The bad news is, it's easy to spend money on them.

Change, Don't Just Switch Seats on the Titanic!

I don't know about you, but if I had not added some new foods to my diet (what I eat, not what I do), I would have been doomed. My weekly indulgences of pizza, fried chicken, pasta, hot wings, large subs, steak tips, rice, burgers, sweet treats and crispy chicken salad with bleu cheese dressing had to stop.

Turning a big ship with a small rudder is not an easy task, especially after its gained half a century of momentum. Realizing that perfection is difficult for even the most committed health and fitness nerds, it is recommend that instead of quitting certain foods and risking a diet failure, that you replace the worst offenders with something better, for a good start to the process. Then add in as many superfoods as you possibly can, and you are on your way past the iceberg.

Fried Chicken - Fried chicken is loaded with calories, that's why it is finger lickin' good. Colonel Sanders lived until he was 90, but trust me, that is not the norm for people who eat a steady diet of food that is high in cholesterol, saturated fat and trans-fat. Did you know there was a study that set out to prove that fat people hang out with fat people? It might be true: Sanders hired Dave Thomas (Wendy's CEO), to turn his business around! Dave, of course, had bypass surgery. Take it from me: being in the heart center is *no fun at all*.

Replace your fried, sautéed, and baked chicken with grilled skinless chicken breast. You'll be able to eat a larger portion while getting the benefit of more protein and less fat. For you city dwellers, you may purchase counter top electric grills that do a very nice job without setting off the smoke detector. Here's a tip: Just grill a bunch, and then freeze it for the six days a week you don't feel like cooking! For the record, the white meat is lower in calories than the dark meat, while wings have the highest fat content.

I am not a purest, however, I suggest choosing your chicken wisely (all food, for that matter). Many popular brands are *enhanced* with a salt solution. Read the label. Federal law prohibits hormones of any kind; therefore, *hormone free* is not a big deal. This is not true for antibiotics, though. If a food producer claims to sell *antibiotic free chicken*, they must document it. Cage-free doesn't specifically mean the chicken roams free, either. Organic? Chicken must be raised with organic methods starting with their second day of life, as well as have access to the outdoors all year round.

Pasta - White flour pasta is another suicide mission, but it's a cheap one. The problem is that it doesn't have a great amount of nutritional value, and it's easy to eat way too much of it. White flour can wreak havoc with both your blood sugar and LDL cholesterol. Instead of white flour pasta, use whole grain/whole wheat pasta if you insist on keeping it on your menu. When you are ready, I recommend replacing it altogether with steamed veggies, brown rice or quinoa!

Wings - I looked up the nutritional value of deep fried Buffalo wings at my favorite local chain. On the website it simply said, "Eat responsibly; a steady diet of fried food is not heart healthy." No kidding, Einstein. Besides, they contain large quantities of fat, sodium, and a measure of protein. It's hard to give up the taste. I am sure eagle's wings are much better for you, but they are tougher to catch because they can actually fly and they can defend themselves. Darwinism at its best.

I suggest replacing them with nitrate free bacon (pork or turkey) wrapped sea scallops or water chestnuts. You can skip the bleu cheese, cut the sodium in half, and the water chestnuts are an inexpensive substitute for scallops. Just drop them under the boiler for about 10 minutes, and you'll be eating before the delivery man can find his car keys. If you must have wings, choose the boneless ones made from breast meat.

Large Sub Sandwiches - Portions people, *portions*! Size *does* matter! All the major sub chains have 1,200 calorie sub sandwiches. At half the size you are at about 600 calories, and with some skillfully-picked toppings, you can get you meal down into the 350 to 400 calorie range.

Once upon a time, back in the 1960s, lived a small subway shop in the armpit of New England. By the 1970s, the little subway train that could, had become a successful franchise, offering a 6 foot sub - yes six feet of white bread topped with dressing, lettuce and cold cuts! Although some of the clientele became obese from the cold-cut-combo and mayonnaise, the train conductors become a bunch of left-wing capitalists serving up so called *healthy* options, while still offering heart-clogging submarine sandwiches. For you and me, the story does not end happily ever after. The tip of the day? Order sandwiches when you need too, and know your ingredients!

Good replacements for any sandwich are foods that are un-processed, nutrient-rich and calorie-sparse. When I don't have left-overs, a few of my favorites include hard-boiled eggs with salsa, tabbouleh salad with lemon, chick pea salad, homemade (where you control the ingredients) soups and vegetarian chili made from salt-free diced tomatoes, black beans, chopped onion and salsa.

Hamburgers - Even the leanest hamburgers on earth are not as healthy as a number of other options. There are hundreds of fast food moguls that are six-feet under! Even the world's best tasting burgers at Five Guys and White Castle are contenders for high-cal-orie, artery-clogging deliciousness. At about 600 calories or more, with bacon and mayonnaise, there are better choices! I am not say-ing that you should *never* enjoy a great burger, but plan your day accordingly.

If you want to know where the beef is, I found it at my local Whole Foods Market, and at a local farm. The ground, grass-fed beef is far lower in saturated fats than the standard 90/10% you get at the supermarket. By blanketing your burger with a 100-calorie whole wheat roll, a few rings of fresh onion, some chopped mushrooms, a slice of avocado or tomato, and topping it with a teaspoon of mustard and a dash of ketchup, you are in business for about 350 to 400 calories. Sneak on a slice of bacon, and you are *still* at 425 net calories!

I suggest replacing beef hamburgers with veggie burgers, which can reduce your consumption of red meat (which is linked to some cancers). They come in a pretty wide variety, and they are lower in net calories and fat. Except for the sodium, it's a pretty good meal!

Crispy Chicken Salad with Bleu Cheese Dressing - Crispy anything is of Satan! The bleu cheese? It's just one of his merry little band of demons. Sure, grilled chicken is good, and low-cal dressing is much better, but salad isn't always filling. How about baked veggies, chickpea casseroles or ratatouille? Looking for something to toss together? How about some chilled and grilled salmon with avocado salsa?

Pizza - Depending on the toppings, it's a killer at 240 to 800 calories *per slice*. It is fortunate that Michelangelo read an early draft of this book before he created his famous statue, "David", otherwise Mike would have made David look more like Buddha. (Apparently he didn't take Viagra, either).

Whole wheat pizza just ain't right. I suggest replacing pizza night with spaghetti night - whole grain, whole wheat spaghetti. Top it with tomatoes (use the low sodium, no-sugar-added kind), and a little bit of goat cheese (less sodium, lower in calories), and even a little bit of lean meat or chicken, if you desire. You can have more toppings with a less carbohydrate-filled base.

Sweet Treats - This is a tough one. Sugar rots your teeth, makes your kids hyper, and causes cancer in laboratory rats. I know... I love it too! I switched to fresh fruit with a teaspoon of low-cal whipped topping, and occasionally a few small pieces of dark chocolate.

Out of Control

Eating out is expensive, but in this busy day and age, it is probably necessary, but avoiding high-calorie food options and oversized portions is nearly impossible when you do. In some states, restaurants are required to list calorie counts on their menus. According to some studies, it is true that consumers make more educated choices about calories because of this. All restaurant chains have to make nutritional information available; check the web before you leave your house or hotel room. There are some restaurants that do not offer *any* complete meals that are 600 to 800 calories.

Even when you choose meals that have lower calorie counts, it can still be easy to overeat. From the first few moments, you'll need to be on your toes. Skip the sweetened and alcoholic drinks and order water, or sparkling water with lemon or lime. This will save 200 or more calories depending on the glass size and whether or not you get refills. Next, skip the breadbasket. Each portion is about 100 calories, sometimes more!

Your first bites should probably be salad, but watch out for the salad dressing. Even low-calorie dressings can be a few hundred calories per serving. Always ask for it on the side. Poor choices in dressing, croutons and nuts can make a small salad bloat to over 500 calories! Next, keep an eye on the carbohydrates! White potatoes and white rice have more than a healthy dose, but the count intensifies by adding butter and sour cream. If it is possible, order a double portion of greens, or substitute brown rice and/or sweet potatoes. I am not a fan of diet butter substitutes, therefore I suggest using real butter if you must.

Your main course will often be enough for two, so think about immediately wrapping half of it up for the dog. Choose meals that are grilled, broiled, or steamed, being sure to avoid fried and sautéed selections.

Dessert? I suggest skipping it. You are easily looking at 300 to 1,000 calories.

Take-out can create the same problems, but you might just want to order a kid's meal or an appetizer. They are smaller portions of the full-size meals, and they'll save you a few bucks too.

Special occasions come at least a few times a year. Holidays, birthdays, entice-your-mate-to-sex day, and anniversaries dot the timelines of life. I am thoroughly against cheat days, cheat meals, and fad diets. There is hardly a dieter who has not fought the good fight and lost the weight only to gain it all back again because they did not make a *life change*. So roll with the days where there is more food than Wal-Mart has walking fashion rebels, and apply the same sort of rules to your own life. Watch the bread, the drinks, and the desserts, while sticking to the rest of the guidelines.

Exterminate

If your furnace was spitting out toxic levels of carbon monoxide, you'd get a new one...right? If you had ants in the kitchen, you'd exterminate them...right? So, why do we keep a pantry full of high calorie, nutrient-sparse snack food and various other junk? "It's not all for me", you say. "It's for the kids!" Well, then, do *them* a favor and toss it! Purge, baby, purge!

CHAPTER ELEVEN

Personal Records

I don't believe anyone who is passionate about any endeavor in life truly understands why they gravitate to the object of their passion. The motivation, the drive to succeed, the love of competition, the personal sacrifice, and depth of the un-interpretable impressions swirling in their spirit like a cool summer breeze, can rarely be described in words. Actually, none of that is true at all; runners are primarily motivated by personal records, "PR" as it's known in the business.

Not all the people who read this book will understand why a runner runs. I don't understand why knitters knit, all babies are cute, or cat people like choking on hairballs. I don't know *why* humans do a lot of things. I have a million questions about stuff I don't understand. Why are the pits in avocados so big? Can vegans eat animal crackers? What if a pescatarian doesn't like fish? How come most people with food allergies are allergic to milk, seafood, and peanuts, which are good for you, and not sugar, fat, and salt, which are not? The record books are full of people who have jumped higher, run farther and faster, eaten more hotdogs in one sitting, and marathon-ed marathons since the first records were kept. Only *they* know why they love what they love.

Runners however, are an unusual type of athlete. Not only do they run (which is often a dreaded drill or punishment in any other sport – can you say "laps" and "wind sprints"?), they are always comparing themselves using two popular methods: pace per mile/kilometer and brightly-colored running shoes.

Photo by: Unknown Runner

October 28, 2012
The Ashland Half Marathon and 5K. This is me at Marathon Park, the original starting line of the Boston Marathon.

Not only do runners often get up extra early and run a few hours on their day off, they tape their nipples, change naked in parking lots on race day, endure being 15-thousandth in line at a porta-potty, crush their privates with compression shorts and sports bras, and to get a little extra speed, they smear Vaseline on their crotch. They don't get whistles, timeouts, half-times, short shifts, a chance to coast, or substitutions from the bench. This hearty bunch endures a host of common injuries from shin splints to stress fractures. And the worst possible injury, a time clock at the finish line which ticks past the thirty-minute or hour mark by a lousy second. For non-runners, please note, it is important to finish a race such as a 5K (3.1 miles), in 29:59 or less. A 10K (6.2 miles) race must be finished in 59:59 or less, a half-marathon in 1:59:59 or less, and a full marathon in 3:59:59 or less. Missing the mark by a tenth of a second is like Robin Hood missing the apple on a man's head by being a few inches low - except we are the guy with the apple on his head!

The one who runs, competes against the clock. This makes no sense to the commoners. It's been said that they'll scoff at paying $10 for a movie ticket, but drop $30 or $40 on a race they hope will last thirty minutes or less.

A runner can't have a "personal record" for a specific distance race until they have run it two or more times. Prior to a second run, it's considered a "best time". Metaphorically speaking, you can't have a favorite child unless there are at least two.

Stories of personal records and injuries are the favored fare of the runner's impassioned table talk. The average runner has a common quirk when it comes to choosing topics to converse about in social situations. When gathering with others to run (please note: training runs are supposed to be slow enough where you can carry on a conversation), this is the favored venue to talk about: work, relationships, kids, that time of the month – about life in general. Conversely, when these same runners gather at any other function, usually involving food and beer, they talk about running. This of course was an observation made by a non-running significant other who thinks running is boring! Behavior of this sort angers everyone, but the blissfully clueless runner. And they wonder why no one wants to come see them finish a race.

Another tendency that these passion-propelled athletes have is to act a little like children under certain circumstances. As in any other sport, there are victories and disappointments. The average runner, well, they are used to losing every race. If only one racer can be first, we can easily surmise a lot of people lose; sometimes hundreds, sometimes thousands.

There is a reason. The idiot race promoters always pay some elite super-human track star to headline the race and crush the rest of us. Therefore, an extremely large population of flailing bipeds, are accustomed to finishing behind someone else. The real problem, other than the clock, is that spilling a three-dollar sports drink is like a child at a carnival losing a helium-filled balloon to a hungry sky.

In achieving a PR, it's important to have a strategy and a training plan. "Run 'til you puke" is not a very workable strategy. "Run 'til you *almost* puke", is. Learning when you've reached that exact moment that you will perform reverse peristalsis on the racecourse is where the training comes in. This is sort of the "barf threshold" for laymen.

Most distance runners cannot believe they can run long distances until they actually do it. Training plans for any race over five miles rarely have you run the full distance before your planned race! A marathoner usually runs a twenty-mile trek as their longest run before they are herded into a corral at the starting line. It is one of the reasons that novice runners like the Disney races; they can slink away in the Mickey Mouse parade if they fail.

It's hard to remember that any accomplishment, whether big or small, is a bridge over the chasm of *defeat*. The truth is that if completing a long distance race was common, there would be no need for the runner to post such unbecoming photographs on social media once their race is completed. Think about it. You come prancing in from mowing the lawn on a hot and humid summer day; perspiration is dripping from your brow, something akin to a sweaty Rorschach Test on the front of your shirt, and your loved one snaps a picture of you and then promptly uploads it to Facebook. You would slap them, am I right?

Sweaty race pictures? You tag yourself, of course.

But what is the runner's worst trait? Self-doubt!

Why 5K Races are a Gateway Drug

Ashland is a little town 26.2 miles from downtown Boston. In fact, in the center of town is the original location of the Boston Marathon starting line. There are two races there every October, one is a 5K (3.1 miles) and the other is a half marathon (13.1 miles). I started training for the "half". Having already run three 10K races and a half dozen 5Ks, it was just another rung up the ladder.

One beautiful September afternoon, I rode my motorcycle over to reckon the course before I committed to signing up for the race (I like to know what I am getting myself into). I was familiar with some of the roads in Ashland, but when I turned onto Green Street, all I could say was Holy Hills! The road would have made a great water park ride; the fast kind that turns your bathing suit into a thong (read: wedgie)! In fact, the course had a lot of hills, a lot of *big* hills! Black gold, Texas tea – sorry, I got a little carried away with the theme to the "Beverly Hillbillies".

Most of my training up to that point had been on relatively flat roads and the high school track near my home. Did I mention that I had a knee injury from running too fast down a hill? I decided I would put my dream of running a half marathon on hold until a flatter course fit my schedule. That, and deep down, I really didn't think I could make it all the way to the finish. Life is like that sometimes. There are many things that we want to accomplish, but when we realize the effort required to actually complete it, we can become overwhelmed. On an even deeper level, we are forced to face our own limitations. It can be illuminating and humbling at the same time.

When I returned home, I got online and registered for the 5K, the shorter distance. At that point, I felt comfortable that I could easily finish a 5K. In the back of my mind I thought I might even secure the coveted PR because most of the course was flat.

I showed up early on race day, had some coffee, a bagel and hobnobbed with a guy I knew from a fitness site I belonged to. I was feeling stoked, confident, I could see myself gracefully breaking the tape at the finish line with my arms in the air. Yeah, I was ready.

We eventually went to the starting line, and like the Charmin bears doing the potty dance (sans the butt-wiggling part), we jogged in place waiting for the announcements to be over and the starting horn to go off.

In 1897 when the Boston Marathon was held there, it was a dirt road, the shoes were not brightly colored, and the starting gun was real. So much had changed, but the heart-pounding anticipation of the race, that was most likely the same.

Bang! Off we went down the road like a snake swallowing its prey. The gaggle of neon-clad runners moved at an ever-increasing pace. Concentrating on my breathing, I finally settled in at a comfortable race pace. I could see my comrade a few hundred yards ahead. In fact, every time I run with Brian, all I get to see is his backside.

One of the things that I love about running is that you ultimately reach a place that is much like being caught in an ocean current, one that can only be mastered by flowing with it. It is a surreal world where your body is functioning in perfect unison with all the elements. The pace is too fast to think deeply, yet, it brings an amazing sense of peace – a sort of nirvana – for about one mile. But then you still have over two more to go. You start feeling your feet pounding the pavement, your muscles begin to scream for more oxygen, and your mind begins to survey the body for fatigue. Odd little pains crop up everywhere only to be outdone by the next one.

Up the hill and on the other side, I could see a meandering line of those ahead of me.

Trying to ignore the pain and fatigue, I pressed on.

It's too fast to slow down for a water stop; I bypassed it in hopes of gaining a few seconds. My lungs were pumping like a freight train with a full load of coal, and my legs were on fire like a rising phoenix. Rounding the last turn, I could see the finish line far in the distance. Calculating my final push, I ran even harder. Listening to my foot-falls, I tried to outpace the footsteps clamoring behind me, real or imaginary, to keep my place in the standings. Maybe I could catch up with the next runner ahead, maybe even pass him by the time I got to that finish line.

Pushing myself, I ramped up the final kick, two-hundred yards to go, then just one-hundred yards: it's a sprint to the timing mat with runners at either elbow.

Finally, I bounded across the finish line, running so fast, I never had a chance to look at the clock, for the moment, I didn't really care. My shoes were braking quickly and I eventually came to a stop hanging onto a guardrail, gasping for air. I felt like vomiting, my legs were hardly able to hold me up, and then I thought to look back at the clock.

Walking back to the staging area I began to think of all the things I might have done differently. We're always our own worst critics, right?

But, hey, I made it! I finished!

The official times were printed and posted on a board at the after party. 25:08. Suddenly, just finishing wasn't quite the reward I thought it was just hours before: the quest for "faster" was on.

Hills for Idiots — "Groton Road Race 10k"

In the pastoral rolling hills of Groton, Massachusetts — forget that. The hills in Groton are steep as hell, where decades ago a sadistic racecourse designer had laid out a course on the outskirts of that quaint little New England village. There are news reporters gathered looking for a story – one which will make sense of the Boston Marathon bombing tragedy just thirteen days before. The band played classic rock, the smell of fresh fruit and meat cooking on gas grills filled the air, while spectators in brightly-colored out-

April 28, 2013

I am not typically thrilled about midday starts, but I had driven by there so many times going to church, I just had to register! It was hot for April, but I would still give it everything I had.

Photo by: Squannacook River Runners

fits began to line the sidewalks and school grounds in anticipation of race day!

As always, I arrived early to make sure I knew where to park, to locate a bathroom (at fifty-something, that's high on the priority list), and to find the check-in table where the race bibs would be handed out. Receiving my race bib and assuring the volunteer that is exactly how to spell my last name (no, the "s" is silent) is the last detail before heading to the starting line – well, after a visit to the restroom.

I have developed a routine for getting ready to race. There is a mental list which I check thirty-one times because I have A.D.D. Forgetting needed items is a hard-learned lesson. One time I had to preach in a small church in Vermont. I brought my suit and tie, and my favorite underwear and dress socks. I did forget a couple of things like deodorant and a tooth brush which was easily found at the local pharmacy. I also forgot shoes, so I had to wear flip-flops with my worsted wool suit. I grew up in Connecticut and live in Massachusetts, so this was a crisis for me (a failure of propriety and church etiquette), forgetting that in Vermont churches it's really no problem, but still I stayed behind the pulpit until everyone left. If you're confused about running and church in the same paragraph, that is what it is like for me to live with A.D.D.

So, to avoid any repeat of such mortification, I ran through the list before the race in the parking lot. Shoes, check. Sun screen, check. Sunglasses…where the hell are my sunglasses!?

On my head, check.

Body glide, on my crotch, check. Car keys, pinned in my shorts pocket with my lunch money, check. Checklist completed, I anxiously headed in the direction of five or six other runners. At the edge of the parking lot there was a fence where we stopped and looked at each other (because it's illegal to be the first one to talk in New England, though it's usually not a breach of protocol to be the first to grunt). Finally a foreigner spoke up. "Does anyone know how to get to the school?" In the distance I saw some runners with Groton Road Race t-shirts from 2012; the previous year's race. "Let's follow them." I said, as I pointed. The New Englanders nodded in agreement and the foreigner said, "Good idea." Thank God that was over — the ice was broken.

Just outside the school gymnasium where the bib pick-up was, I bumped into Brian, a guy that I had seen at a number of races. Brian was one of my heroes, having lost of over 240 pounds through diet and exercise. That was one of me that he lost – an entire overweight adult! We chatted a bit, and I got my bib. I looked over the free t-shirt which everyone gets for their $50 entry fee. To date, Brian has smoked me in the 5K, the 10K, the 10-miler, and the half marathon. With a fifteen year age difference as a handicap, I win them all.

It was hot, and the temperature at start time was seventy degrees Fahrenheit. We milled around the starting line and chatted with the runners that were not in Zen Yoga meditation poses. On the side of the track was a local reporter looking for a post "Boston Marathon Bombing"story, and we talked about that for a while. The small talk ended with announcements which no runner likes — not ever. Then the "Star Spangled Banner" was sung by a local high school student. I confess, I usually zone out because my mind is in race-mode by that time. But with the tragedy in Boston still fresh in my mind, it was a very emotional moment.

I'm not a fast runner, nor am I a slow runner. I am best classified as a half-fast runner (yeah, I'm a "glass-half-full kinda guy). That, coupled with the fact that I get to the starting line with my shorts on the right way around and my shoes tied (thank God for that checklist!), was really a miracle. Most races start with an air horn, but this one uses a cannon. In fact, there were a lot of apologies for the fact it might sound like a bomb going off, but we won't let a couple of terrorists take away our traditions, the cannon would still signal this race as it always had.

The pack of about a thousand runners inched forward, strained and waiting for that signal. I wished my friend Brian a good race, popped in my headphones, and started my GPS run-tracking app on my phone.

Boom! And we were off.

Over the timing mat I jumped ahead and took to the outside. There are always lots of slower runners trying to get road position so they can speed up to race pace. In some races, the first mile is nearly a walk. I ran on top of a flat curb on the edge of the track and then found some room on the wide driveway down to the first turn onto Main Street.

I settled into my preplanned pace of 9:45 per mile. There are lots of race strategies, but mine is to maintain a steady pace for the entire journey. Off in the distance, I could see Brian pulling away. I smiled for the photographer as we headed through the village (it's an instinctive thing, I can't help it). I felt good, my pace felt right, and I started thinking about "The Boston" — I was in my zone.

The first of many rolling hills began. I used my bounding Kenyan hill technique. Who knew that inside this fat white guy was an inner-Kenyan crying out? Most runners complain about hills like football fans complain about bad referee calls. I don't mind them because it means that there is a downhill somewhere in my future. I pick up the pace on the next series of downhills, and cross the two-mile mark at 18:03. This is well below my anticipated 19:30. My goal is to finish ten kilometers (6.1 miles) in under an hour.

Pleased with my race so far, I sped on to the first water stop. Water is a choking hazard, so I took a quick rinse and dumped the rest on my head to cool off. I rounded the corner, and there before me was the legendary Big Kahuna, a hill with ascent of 327 feet in less than a half mile. It's a little discouraging, but I leaned into it and attack it like any other hill — just a lot more of it. Passing dozens of walking runners, I pressed on. Half way up the hill, one of the town's folk has placed a lawn sprinkler by the road, as he watches us enjoy the cooling waters of life from his farmers' porch.

I decided to take a walk break. I know that I am ahead of my planned pace, passing the four-mile mark nearly four minutes ahead of schedule. For one hundred yards, I caught my breath and recalculated my strategy.

Finally having ascended to the top, I was looking forward to all those downhills to the finish line. After a slight downhill, around the corner there was another long, slow incline.

What the heck!?

I pushed myself ahead, but I could start to feel my heart racing, and my legs getting heavier. I decided to take a two hundred yard walk break. A hint of discouragement set in. I don't really know what my pace was, or what my walk break was going to cost me. This is the mental part of running a race, and I have to admit, I'm sort of a wuss. I started going through the motions thinking that my sub-hour 10K was slipping away.

It was hot, I was tired, and I was the only one that cared about my time.

At the top of the hill, a man in a red tech-t passed me. I had seen him on and off throughout the race. I can beat him, I thought, (he looked a lot older than me!). So I leaned into the hill. My run app chirped my five mile time of 49:38. Before me was a water stop and another downhill. I passed the man in red, skipped the water stop, and sped up to take advantage of my good fortune. As I strode down a long, easy decline I could hear the band playing near the finish line. It seemed like forever before we rounded that last corner onto the oval track.

One hundred yards to the last corner, a few hundred feet in the corner, and fifty yards to the timing mat. I gave it everything I had, but there wasn't much left. I passed a man being held up by emergency medical technicians and saw another in the first-aid tent on oxygen. I passed a few people, but then a woman went streaking by me.

I could swear I heard the announcer on the public address speakers saying, "Johndrow is being beaten by a *woman* (again!), he's going to have a lot of 'splaining to do!"

I could see the clock and it said 59:27 in the distance and I gave it my last push. By the time I had caught my breath, the clock was well past one hour. I held myself up against the fence, gasping for air. My legs were like Jell-O; the kind that can't be nailed to a tree. Brian met me there to congratulate me. Another friend got me bottle of water and I found a banana to eat.

Did I make it? Did I do it in under an hour? I just didn't know for sure.

Finally, I decided to walk around a little and took the medical tape off my nipples. I thought, why is it that the same tape that peels your skin off in the hospital, ends up in your running shorts when you use it to tape your nipples? I don't have an answer. I got a hamburger from the grill and walked down to look at the print out of times.

My chip time was *59:08*! I had done it!

The party was winding down, and I walked back to my car with a genuine sense of accomplishment. Having a personal record doesn't always come with fanfare, medals or even a high-five at the finish line. What happens is deep in the soul of a runner. It overflows a well that can forever bring a quiet smile to your face and provide social media posts that only another runner will understand.

Competing Against Yourself

Long-time friends Scott and Cindy came to visit me yearly so that Cindy could run the Boston Marathon. The long distance between Virginia and Massachusetts made the race a perfect time for us to connect and spend some time together.

In 2013, Cindy was unable to make it for the annual big event in my backyard – missing the bombings. We decided, instead, that year I would visit them in Virginia. I asked Cindy to pick a race that we could run together, and she chose the "Crawlin' Crab Half Marathon" in Hampton. I booked a flight using my frequent flyer miles, and off I went for a long weekend.

Scott and I drank oceans of coffee, watched Eric Clapton's *Crossroads* video, and talked about everything from religion and politics to kids and retirement. He also listened to Cindy and I do what runners do best, talk about running in the presence of non-runners, as if they're at all interested (but we really don't care).

Scott is very supportive, and made every effort to make sure the two of us had everything we needed on race day. We left the

October 6, 2013

Ran the Crawlin' Crab Half Marathon in Virginia with my long time friend Cindy White. I had been friends with her husband for nearly thirty years. Look at me; I am going to be as famous as Curt Schilling with his bloody sock because of a bloody left nipple.

house with a cooler full of drinks and equipment bags with our race stuff. As we stepped into the car, the temperature was in the high sixties. The temperature at the start was supposed to be in the low seventies — all with the dreaded 98% humidity. There was not a cloud in the sky; there would be plenty of nice, hot sunshine.

It's always nice to find yourself in that happy place with your race bib in hand, the car parked, and a short line at the porta-potty. It's called runner's bliss.

I wished Cindy Godspeed. Taking a short jog around the parking lot to warm up, good luck wishes from Scott, and I headed for my corral. In it there were hundreds of runners getting in their respective zones. I looked around for runners I thought would be at my pace — usually the older ones in wheelchairs with green oxygen tanks hanging on the handlebars. Ahead of me was the two-hour-pace team, while not far behind was the two-hour-and-ten-minute team. The pacers are experienced runners who can finish in a prescribed amount of time. They run a very even race, which is my kind of race. I need a finish time of less than two hours and fourteen minutes for a PR. I already knew it was too hot to finish in two hours. In fact, my last half marathon I had been on pace for a two hour and thirteen minute finish when I got a leg cramp that had me walking on and off for the last three miles.

This was another chance for a PR. In life we need to keep in mind an occasional defeat is temporary, but giving up is a permanent condition.

I am *not* a quitter.

I toed the starting line. The heat of the day was far from my thoughts as I waited for my corral to start the race. And then, we were off.

I took an easy pace, and waved to Scott who stood along the railing of the police barrier. I looked ahead into the sea of runners and just stuck to my pace. The course was flat, flat as a table top. I thought that this should be easy because there are no hills to slow me down, but I forgot that there were also no downhill stretches either.

I'll spare you the boring details. It was hot (did I mention, it was hot?). Yeah, really hot.

The water stops were more a place to cool off with a cup of water on my head than to get refreshed. I stayed on pace with a fellow named Michael. "You talk, I'll breathe." I said, knowing that every breath now, meant life-giving strides later. We ran together until mile eight, down by the ocean and the jelly bean stop. He went on ahead as we turned up a shaded street. Let me say that Virginia is nothing like Massachusetts. There on the route, was a man smoking. I asked him if I could have one, and then invited him to come on and run with me. And what is that in the distance, a mirage? It was a full bar with beer, wine, and mixed drinks at which there was a waiting line. "Thank you Hampton!" I shouted as I went by.

At the end of the street, it was back out into the sunshine. A few hundred feet ahead of me were the two-hour-and-ten-minute-pacers. I sped up slowly to get back on pace. The hot miles wore on as the clock ticked away. I ran with another fellow named, Michael. He was having some trouble, and I could hear his heart monitor saying that he was 165 beats per minute. Mine was at 157. For middle-aged guys this is not sustainable with three miles to go. (Individual heart rates may vary a lot more than the standard charts state.)

I was not concerned about my heart, but my heart rate was high again after just a few more minutes, a sign that my body was starving for oxygen. My experience is that this is the beginning of the end. Off in the steamy distance were the two-ten-pacers and passing me were the two-fifteens. Because this race uses chip time (from start mat to finish mat, not from the starting gun), you never know exactly where you are. It's wise to continue with your best effort, especially if you started back a few hundred yards.

As we approached an overpass, the only hill on the entire course, many of the runners were complaining. I chuckled to myself. My driveway in the Worcester Hills is steeper than that, I thought. The heat was beginning to take its toll on the runners, as a number of ambulances passed us on the race route. Just a few weeks before, a man died in the heat and humidity at another Virginia half marathon.

I took a few more walk breaks; that day was just not going to turn out to be a personal best. In fact, it was going to be my slowest half marathon of the three I'd done thus far.

At mile thirteen I felt the presence of God, and for the next few hundred yards I simply enjoyed that. On the last corner there was a young woman with a Boston Strong t-shirt. She gave me a high-five as I passed by — for whatever reason — and I shed a few tears.

As I came closer to the finish line, I sped up. There is no sense finishing with anything left to give. A few hundred yards before my friends Scott and Cindy cheered me on. "Go David!" I gave it everything I had, and passed a number of runners as I faintly heard my name on the P.A. My run application confirmed a speed of 13.25 miles per hour (4:32 pace). I pulled up to the nearest crowd barrier and hung on. A race marshal came over to ask if I was alright. "I need water and some shade", I said without looking up. My partners came over to congratulate me on a finish.

"David, you are bleeding." Cindy said. I just looked down and connected my burning left nipple with the blood stain on my sweat-drenched white running shirt. I was too exhausted to care, though.

After I changed in the parking lot at the Hampton Roads Convention Center, we stopped for a seafood lunch and pretty much talked about running until Scott's ears bled.

Runners. Go figure.

CHAPTER TWELVE

Winning the War

Most of us fantasized about being in a relationship with a famous movie or TV personality, or a musician or sports figure at some point in our lives — and it wasn't Roseanne Barr! That is what the wonderful thing about fantasy is, it's free, but often not fulfilling, and after a long time, draining.

Losing inches and getting down to a healthy weight does not have to be a fantasy. Fitness, despite the battle, is worth it. *You can do it!* Lots of people have done it — really! I read amazing success stories about people like you and me that have lost literally tons of fat (without cutting off their heads). It can be done.

I don't know about you, but I get tired of skinny people telling me how to do it, are you with me? Just eat less, blah blahblah.To quote Bill the Cat, another great statesman of our time: "Ack!".

Of course they can eat a half of a freakin' pizza and down a liter of Coke — 1600 calories for lunch — and it doesn't show up on the scale, or their hips, their butts, or make their thighs rumble and roll when the walk. But you and me, we are not like that. We eat one extra slice of pizza and grow another chin overnight. Hell, we eat a big meal and have to loosen our belts and start responding to elephant mating calls. Being fat sucks! Can I get a witness!?

One thing though, in the "plus" column: The invention of stretch-waist pants saved our lives.

So how does a Willy the wallowing whale become a flippin', er, Flipper the sleek dolphin? It starts with what you do and ends with what you think. I know, it seems backwards!

You Haven't Tried Everything, So Don't Lie!

If you were ever like me, you've probably felt trapped by a stubborn body. Maybe it wouldn't lose weight, maybe it wouldn't move as fast as your running buddy, or maybe you just felt tired and old. When you feel like that for any length of time, it's hard to beat the voices in your head telling you that for today, sitting on the couch in your PJs is as good as it gets — especially if you have a tray of chocolate truffles and a bottle of champagne.

In the years since my health and fitness epiphany, I've heard "I've tried everything!" more than Prince Charming had suitors at the royal ball. A lot of times, it was my own voice that I heard saying it. But, I don't believe it anymore. What you are saying is, everything you have tried has failed. The fact is this: Lots of people beat the fat gene.

I am pretty sure that you haven't eaten an ox from a box or a dog in the fog. And it's doubtful that you have eaten an egg with your leg. Sorry, I was reading Dr. Seuss to my little one as I ~~penned~~ typed this chapter.

The first step to success is to clean house. Take a look around the cabinets, the pantry, the desk drawer, glove box, underwear drawer (edible undies are fattening) and the root cellar. I am sure you can find food that is unhealthy. Toss it, have a party and let your friends eat it, or have a bon fire — but whatever you do, get rid of it. The killers are leftover birthday cake, large bags of chips that demand to be finished, and a host of other demonic treats, sweets, and fatty foods.

Try new foods, new recipes and adding superfoods. You'll need to find new favorite dishes; most of mine include bacon (sweet, crispy, heavenly…uh, sorry), in small amounts, it is a tasty ingredient. We have a favorite cauliflower dish that uses red pepper flakes, pine nuts, lemon juice, garlic and oregano. Adding in fruits and vegetables along with other whole grains, low fat dairy and lean meat can really make a difference.

The basic formula for success is more calories out than in. For some, getting fit is less about food and more about exercise. Take every opportunity to do more things which burn calories. I really do park as far from the door as possible. I still snicker at the road-rage in the YMCA parking lot over the front row spot. Everyone needs a shorter walk to the treadmill. I always take the stairs (yes, I got stuck in an elevator once, but that is not why). I have a push lawn mower, I bike to the store for a few things, I stand at the kitchen counter and cut my veggies and fruit instead of buying them, and I dance with my kid instead of watching TV. It's not pretty, I will admit that, but I am dressed. Steps count, use them to your advantage.

Shop smart! If you need to use an interior aisle in the grocery store or supermarket, it is probably processed (and the security cameras are aimed there too in case you are short on cash)! Fruits, veggies, fresh meat, fish, produce, dairy, and fresh bakery are almost always found on the perimeter aisles. Skip the canned foods, cereal, cookies and pet food aisles — it's tough to do while you're right there in the trenches, but later, you'll be glad you did.

Size matters, but no one ever talks about it. We are a family of two adults and one child. The older children are now fending for themselves and took the damn pretzels and Pepsi with them! It's hard to buy anything that is a good portion size for the three of us. Me, I hate to have the same thing two days in a row if I can help it. In our house we freeze stuff: Meat, fish, poultry, lunches, dinners, and one time even the cat (but that was an accident; he was pretty ticked when we thawed him out, now he just sits on top of the fridge and leers at us like a vulture). We also buy nuts in bulk and keep the plastic jars for other stuff like Barbie shoes.

We have small plates and super small tubs for packing lunch in. It's an optical illusion, but two cups of veggies and a four ounce piece of salmon looks like plenty of food.

Mindless grazing is another dietetic time bomb waiting to go off when you step on the scale. It happens when eating is not the focus of your activity. Weight-loss experts suggest only eating at the table, not while cooking, sitting at your desk, watching television or sitting in the living room. And come on, not in the bedroom, someone is going to have to sleep on those cracker crumbs! Can't you think of something else to do in your bedroom? Besides, do you really want the dog rooting around looking for bits of saltines at 2:00 in the morning?

TV Aerobics, sometimes called "couch cardio", is the new fad. If you use the tube for an hour a day, you get approximately twelve minutes of commercials. Instead of going to the kitchen for a snack during a commercial, do some squats, leg raises, pushups, sit ups, planks or just stand up and walk around. If you watch two hours, you can fit in a small cardio workout. And if you watch three hours a night, you should get a stationary bike, elliptical or treadmill and train for a marathon!

Get a dog that needs walking. I guess a cat would be alright too — if you are going to chase balls of yarn and ralph up hairballs on your pillow.

The Monk's New Habit

The problem with most diets is three-fold. First, they require that you change so many aspects of your life that they can be overwhelming. The second is that most humans want to do the least amount of work for the greatest amount of reward. And third, the first two cover it nicely.

Changing habits is the fastest way to becoming fit (unless you are a Monk). It requires some concentrated doing, not just good intentions. Choosing new foods that you can and will enjoy eating, and picking some sort of activity that you'll look forward to participating in is a start. Keep in mind that most experts recommend that you exercise doing something that gets your heart rate above 120 to 130 beats per minute for thirty minutes; which, except for the elite, excludes sex. At the very least, for most humans, this is a brisk walk.

Chapter 10 had an extensive food list; that is just a start! There are hundreds of healthy meal recipe websites. Your first new habit could be as simple as skipping the bread when you go out to dinner and saving those calories for another day. Another good idea is to drink a large glass of water before you eat.

Daily habits are the toughest ones to master, but they are essential. The most important habit you can develop is planning a food diary for the week. This allows you to be less focused on managing one meal. Reading the label is an essential building block for making menus which will work for you. Your plan helps prevent impulse meals which you already know how they are going to turn out. If you've got a hot date or a celebration Friday evening, you can put some calories in the bank on Thursday and Friday morning. Rationing your weekly calories is always a good strategy.

The other challenge is adding movement to your day. Even if you have three workout sessions planned each week, there are still four other days to run up the calorie counter. According to an article entitled "Sitting is the New Smoking- Even for Runners" on the Runner's World magazine website, we need to do a lot more during our non active times. How can you improve? Standing is better than sitting, walking is better than standing, running is better than walking and walking pet mice on a leash is hardly worth the effort.

Planning daily activity takes some thought. Finding free spaces in your schedule isn't easy, but most of us have them, if you look hard enough. Spend a little time analyzing your day, maybe you have two fifteen minute breaks where you can grab a coffee and walk around the block, hit the stairs for a dozen flights, or just walk from one end of the building to the other. Stay-at-home parents can take the stroller around the block with junior, or walk the perimeter of the playground while the kids play with a cinder block in the stroller for ballast. Most of us get a lunch break, and the best way to spend it is walking, at the corporate gym, or the treadmill at the local YMCA. Most experts agree that the cumulative activity is as good as one thirty minute workout. Plan on getting up from your chair as often as you can. And please note: drinking eight or more cups of water a day (as you should do anyway) can provide you with a good reason to get up!

The successful not only plan to succeed, but they succeed at planning.

Rock 'Em, Sock 'Em Thoughts

I can't. — If you are telling yourself that there is some reason you just can't lose weight, you can't run, or you can't be fit, you probably won't ever be! Regardless of your perception of your habits and self-image (which I believe was created in God's image), your mind is at war with everything that you need to do to become healthier and fitter. Even those with handicaps and disabilities have completed marathons.

I'm too busy. — Most everyone is busy with something that makes it difficult to focus on health and fitness. It is something that you have to *make* time for. If working out is not in your calendar, it is unlikely that you'll win at fitness bingo, *extremely* unlikely. Health and fitness is a choice — now may be the time to make it. Or, as one of my friends is fond of saying, see you at the funeral!

I'm young. — You may be young enough in dog years where your food and lack of exercise is not a problem, but for most it doesn't work forever — especially past age forty. And you may not have as much time as you think. Yeah, I know about your grandmother that drank a case of beer a day, smoked three packs of cigarettes, only ate fried food, dated five men at a time and lived to be thirty-nine. Some of us would like to last a little longer. I also realize that not everyone dies from an unhealthy lifestyle — people also win the lottery and take vacation trips to the International Space Station, too.

Everyone in my family is fat. — Why is that? Could it be diet and exercise (or lack thereof)? Taking charge of what we do will eventually change the way we think.

It's a cheat day. — Get out your stones and excuses about shaking up your metabolism blah blah blah. The truth is that cheaters are in the group of roller coaster dieters, from which nearly all eventually gain back the weight they lost the other six days of the week — and sometimes even more. Think of it like a drug addict smoking a little crack, or your friend being a little pregnant. It is extraordinarily hard for humans to live in this sort of cycle. Eventually centrifugal force reaches a critical stage and things just fall apart.

I can eat whatever I want in moderation. — This is the war cry of those that are probably not ready to make a lifestyle change. Taking charge of your life means that there are food items that need to be dropped from the menu. It also may include a few permanent additions.

I have kids. — So take them for a run. I take my youngest daughter on a mile walk every day that is nice enough to do so. I take her to the park to ride our bicycles for forty-five minutes or more on weekends. We plan vacations near bike trails as well. When she was a baby, we just put her in the front pack or the bicycle trailer. My YMCA has kids care as well.

The dog/kangaroo didn't eat it. — Restaurant doggie-bags can be a savior or a killer. Few restaurants serve a complete meal under a thousand calories. For the average person, this is two meals-worth of food. Instead of being tempted to eat your entire entrée, be sure to have half of it bagged for another time or to bring it home for lunch another day. If you are just going to eat it when you get in from your dinner date, just leave it at the restaurant!

I don't know what to do! — I don't have a degree in health and nutrition. My suggestions are simply a guideline for the amount of food and balance of carbohydrates, protein and fat as well as other essential nutrients that you will need. Here's a tip, if it is low-cal junk food, it's still junk food. If you are eating more than you are burning, you are going to gain weight. If you are not active, you can't eat as much.

It's too hard to lose weight, I've already tried. — You are correct, losing weight is difficult and you've proved it. That is why you make lifestyle changes and don't go on a diet. A lifestyle change requires an adjustment to your life that you can do for the rest of your life.

I can't afford healthy food. — I will agree that a variety of healthy of food is more expensive than a box of pasta and a loaf of white bread. Here are some tips for saving money. Drink only water, it's free. Many grocery stores have fruits and veggies that are discounted because they are past fresh. I have seen six apples for a dollar, two peppers for half a buck, and three bananas for even less. Overall they are a good value. Brown rice is the same price as white, and far better for you. Eggs are a good source of protein and so are garbanzo beans. Because many of us are now eating less, this can save money too. The average portion size of meat, poultry or fish is about four ounces. You can buy larger packages of meat and freeze it — better yet, grill it, then freeze it. The same is true for some fruits and veggies. Frozen food isn't horrible, and most canned food can be rinsed to reduce sodium content.

It's too late. — I can't imagine that, unless you are dying in the next couple of days, that it is never too late to change your diet and achieve some significant health benefits. Whatever age you are today, tomorrow you be that plus one day.

I'm afraid of failure. — I have met many people that have a lot of weight to lose (me, I had to lose close to one hundred pounds). It is a daunting task and it takes time. Reading success stories and engaging with others on the same journey is very helpful. I find others' progress inspiring! On average, those who have fifty to one hundred or more pounds to lose, can expect to safely lose one or more pounds a week. Of course it depends on many factors from age, to diet, genetics and personal effort (yes, I am sure there are some with medical reasons who really can't, but I'm not talking about them). And when it gets down to ten to twenty pounds, things tend to slow way down. The point is that with effort, knowledge, and time, it will eventually work for just about everyone.

I'm afraid of success! — Being obese for a long period of time becomes a way of life. We set up our enablers, buy roomier cars, bigger furniture and even our personality changes to accommodate our physical state. I sat with a fellow from work once who could not fit in the booth at a pizza joint place. Then he ordered a three thousand calories extra large submarine sandwich! It was sad.

My significant other doesn't care, why should I? — Most mature adults are smart enough not to say something as stupid as "I would love you better thinner!" I suppose there are some that have spouses that like them in an unavailable state, but for the most part, our health is our concern. Losing weight has many benefits other than just looking and feeling better.

I can't exercise. — We need to start where we stand. The goal is eating well, and getting in three thirty minute cardio sessions a week in which we get the heart rate over 130. You can walk in place, buy home gym resistance bands, and an array of other inexpensive fitness items. I'll bet you can find a treadmill, stationary bike or elliptical trainer online for cheap! Just do a search on Craig's List for "coat rack".

I love to eat. — Yup, me too! I am just enjoying eating better, and less.

I do a lot of traveling for work and find it hard to stick to my weight loss plan. — It is not an easy task to eat out all the time, but many places I have stayed at had a refrigerator and a nearby grocery store.

I've heard that running puts me at risk for knee problems and arthritis later in life. — I personally think this is baloney! If you drop the weight, use proper running form, and have properly fitted running shoes, you should have very few problems with your joints if you start out slow and increase gradually. If you can't believe that, then swim, use the elliptical, or ride a bike.

It's just one. One breakfast muffin is equal to two thirty minute cardio sessions. You can't out exercise a bad diet.

It's the holidays. — So?

I don't cook my own meals. — It's hard to control what others do. I made an agreement with my wife over what I was willing to eat each week. Communication helps, and filling up with a large snack before meals is also another option. If you eat half a bag of baby carrots, you are probably not going to chow down on the three pieces of fried chicken.

I am not sure I can do all that is required. — I believe that if you don't really want to be fit, you won't be. Worse, you may just have decided that you'll always be fat and you'd be right. Unless you can desire to be fit, from which thinner is a byproduct, it will never happen unless you're stranded on a tofu ranch (I deleted the reference to being tied up and added it to the chapter on sex).

I am not organized. — If your life has no real schedule or structure, it's going to be tough, really tough to live a fit life. Losing weight requires doing the same thing over and over and over and over and over to get the desired result.

Practice not Perfection

It doesn't matter where you go, overweight and obese people have a million excuses for not losing and maintaining a healthy weight. You can call it "grasa", "fett", "gordura" or just plain old "fat", but it is a health hazard by any name.

After my heart trauma, what I heard afterwards shocked me: 57% of those that have had a heart attack don't even continue to take their medication after the first refill! Close to 80% make no significant lifestyle changes. Why? First it is overwhelming. The other reason is that it requires a significant change in your daily routine — ummm — self-discipline.

You don't have to be perfect, but you have to be determined. In fact, I was so bad at this, I'll bet I could have gotten Richard Simmons depressed and Jane Fonda to cry. If you want a date with your favorite entertainer, you need to be attractive enough to get in the game. Me, I just want to please me (and love dates with my wife!). Because I was once thin, that is the picture I have in my own mind. I'd like it to match the *"me"* in the mirror. If you've never been thin, get a role model (some folks clip out a photo from a celebrity magazine and tape it to the fridge, a great reminder as you reach for the door handle to grab a slice of chocolate cake)!

Here Are Some More Tips for Succeeding!

Pick non-food rewards for yourself when you reach short-term goals. If you lose five pounds you give yourself some new music. Lose ten, get an early Christmas present like a new bike. And when you lose twenty-five or fifty, ask your significant other for a new car and a week in Hawaii — unless you already live there, then go to Alaska.

Ask yourself this: If I was thin, what would my life look like? Would it be Charlie Sheen? Paris Hilton? Oprah Winfrey? Bart Simpson? Success ain't all it's cracked up to be, you can change your surroundings and make better food choices now — you just have to do it.

Each one of us has a time when we're most likely to overeat, whether it is the morning coffee break or when we first arrive back at the Bat Cave. You need to plan to handle them and stick to your plan. If you are going to gorge yourself with a much needed snack when you walk in the door after work, think about just eating dinner at that time. If you overeat on coffee break with junk food, have your snack before you get there.

Surround yourself with people who want you to be healthy. Your fat, diabetic, grandmother — the one who pinches your cheek every time she sees you and gets the walking farts in the kitchen — she is probably not the person you want cooking your meals and suggesting dishes for the holidays. Even our good friends can sabotage weight-loss attempts. Not everyone looks at a cookie as a death threat, for you and me, we need to weigh our options carefully, and choose people that are on our team!

Stock your pantry and refrigerator with healthy foods. If you are serious about losing weight, then you need to skip the high-calorie junk. That life is *over!*

Get a mirror, take pictures, drop your dating profile from the Chubby Dates website and make a YouTube video asking your fantasy date out — you never know!

Understanding the Gym Culture

Gyms are interesting places. The YMCA where I live is sort of the Wal-Mart of gyms. It's big, it's got a lot of stuff in a huge building, and the people, let's just say, are colorful. I am going to start a web page "People of the Y", no doubt, you'll see many of the same characters you now see on the "People of Wal-Mart" site, only everyone is dressed in spandex and carrying water bottles.

Come with me on a short journey from desk jockey and couch potato to amateur runner and health nerd, as I share the anatomy of the neighborhood gym.

The Personal Equipment: If you are going to be a health nerd, you need health nerd stuff. First, you need running shoes fitted at a running store. It is best to get the ones that do not have the flashing LED's, Dora the Explorer or Diego on them (seriously, get good ones at a specialty store, not at a department store).

Then you need a musical device; an iPod, smartphone or MP3 player will do. If it's a really sharp-looking gadget, then you'll need to get the Velcro arm band holder for it, so you can share its awesomeness with everyone else at the gym. But there is a practical purpose for the arm band, you don't have to hold it when you use the rest room, and it's harder to drop your device into the toilet because your knees feel like rubber after a workout. If it is a cheesy Barbie phone, you may want to stitch a pocket for it in your drawers to keep it out of sight. Be sure that you have headphones because, at the gym, sharing is *not* caring!

If you are really cool (like the author and editors of this book) you need a heart rate monitor (HRM) to keep track of your pulse, so that you can tell the paramedics what rate it was at when your heart exploded. Some of them have alarms so you know when you are about to die on the treadmill. Mine is wireless and to my surprise, not only does it show up on the special decoder wristwatch

I have as well as my smartphone, but it displayed on the Precor treadmill too. Freaky! Gotta wonder if the NSA had anything to do with that technology? And how much of my workout are they keeping track of. Hmmm....

What's next? A study to show that diet and exercise is the only good way to lose weight?

The Apparel: In the old days we had sweatpants and sweatshirts. Period! Wal-Mart could have saved aisles and aisles if that were still the case — but it's not. Now you can get Spandex (please don't if it makes you look like a package of pork tenderloin!), polyester, fake velvet, and even sequins. I am just kidding about the sequins...I hope.

Here are a few far-outfits that seem a little strange to me.

Shorts-Over: Ok, so sweat pants are not enough, you need to wear gym shorts over them? You should think this over, my daughter is little scared of you.

Tank Tops: These are reserved for a select few, and honestly, you are not one of them. The Bingo Wings are killing me, your Man Boobs are not attractive, and please don't bend over to do pushups!

Street Clothes: For cryin' out loud, it's not casual Friday! I get that you think sweating is just too much work, but try to at least fake it. You're at the gym, not a hardware store.

Leo-Tights: Whoever thought of wearing a leotard over tights was probably very trim and lived close to a bathroom. I think it was Jane Fonda, but you are not her.

Sandals: Leave them in the car with your bong. Please, get some sneakers. I don't care if they have Power Rangers or Ninja Turtles on them, just get some!

Baseball Hats: I know it supports your pony tail, and supposedly keeps sweat out of your eyes, but save it for your kid's soccer field. Men, is this your thinking cap? Get a sweat band that you can wash!

Split-Side Running Trunks: Men, please, you are not Burt Reynolds and your tidy-whities are not all that white. Ladies, unless you have fabulous hips, I would rather not see your cellulite. Deal?

Braless: Assuming you are not 9-years-old, or are applying for a job as a thermometer, keep it (them) to yourself.

Shirtless: This ain't the beach, and you have enough hair on your back to plug two sinks and an old fashioned bath tub. No thanks.

Sports Bra Only: Why are you doing this? You don't have 6-pack abs, and it's not mating season. I am a little confused.

1960's Headphones: Spring for the fifteen bucks and get a sports pair. I promise Sgt. Pepper's Lonely Hearts Club Band will sound even more drug-drenched. Oh right, and from the back, you look like you have a ten pound dumbbell on your shoulders.

Police Academy Sweats: You expect us to believe you are/were a cop? I would like to see your badge.

Water Bottle Fanny Pack: I am not sure why you need that, there are drink holders on all the weight machines, it's not a marathon, and there is a bubbler on the wall. And every time I walk by you, I want to snap it!

I also had no idea you could mix and match maroon wool Scottish plaids and pink velour. Does anyone buy plain black clothes anymore? And what's up with cheap polyester? It makes noise, lots of noise (not like the expensive polyester). The good news is that, if you are huge like I was, you won't be going very fast and you'll be able to keep the noise under 90 decibels! For those of us that still have BMIs in the 20s or 30s, it's a good idea to stay away from the spandex, especially the shiny kind. Besides, that stuff can catch on fire pretty easily. I'm just saying. Oh, and remember, Richard Simmons is not trendy.

The Diet: Come on, you've maybe tried a few such as Jenny Craig, Atkins, South Beach or the Dill Pickle Diet. If you are going to lose pounds, as we've discussed, you need to change the way you eat — there are loads of spices besides chocolate and salt. If you want be cool in the gym, bring muscle milk or a protein shake. Cool at your first 5K? Grab some GU or Cliff bars and Gatorade.

The Music: If you are going to move, you need music. It should rock; you are not meditating for God's sake! I suggest, Led

Zeppelin, Burn Service, Steve Miller, Kutless, Tim Hughes and Jason Aldean.

The Goals: My first was to just run a 5k race, instead I had heart failure, but eventually I got there. You can have weight goals which can be elusive as evolution, measurement goals, or times for events from swimming to biking. It is also good to have fitness and health goals that end up with balanced blood work.

The Apps!   I have a couple of apps on my phone. Noom was my favorite for the first two years. It kept track of all my exercise and food consumption. Since I first started, my needs have changed. I use My Fitness Pal, Fitbit and Endomondo as well as a Garmin GPS.

The People: There are some funny characters in the gym. You've met them, the newbies in their blue jeans and loafers, the front row students in the classes worshipping a trainer, and the posers in front of the mirror in the free-weight room. Don't be one of them, you have a greater purpose, keep that in mind and be humble.

The Dos and Don'ts: Don't stand chatting while you are in front of the membership card readers. Otherwise people have to reach past your rear end to check in.

Never ask to change the TV channel, CNN, Ellen, and CSI, that's as good as it gets! Besides, you are there to exercise. Just turn up your mp3 player and stay focused.

The sign says "NO CELL PHONES" and that means you, genius. Plug in your iPod and sing in your head.

Do I really need to explain boogers?

I know you've worked hard on that body. Striking a bicep pose does not negate the fact that you are 120 pounds overweight. I mean people are still going to see your belly.

Are you going to exercise or not? Forty-five minutes of stretching and walking past a row of exercise machines does not constitute cardiovascular exercise.

Water Fountains: OK, so you needed to spit in there? Why?

A good trainer has that "I can break you in two" look in their eye. Find one!

CHAPTER THIRTEEN

Sex, Men, and Running

Sex

This page intentionally left blank by the author.

Why Men Lose Weight More Easily Than Women, Really

It appears that weight loss is sexist. Most experts, even woman experts, say that men lose weight more quickly and easily than woman. That's not all they do more quickly; it is the microwave-versus-the-crockpot analogy.

I have few thoughts that are shrouded in stupidity, and flavored with, perhaps, a dash of truth.

Clothes: Men don't buy clothes in sizes. If man goes from a size 12 to an 8, it is because he cut off half his foot in a chainsaw accident.

Gastric Bypass (Flatulation): Men just fart more, sometimes significantly reducing their body mass and destroying meaningful conversation at the same time despite any futile efforts of blaming a conveniently adjacent pet (other than goldfish).

Muscle Mass: Men have a few more places to put muscles; for example, the mouth (please refer to an anatomy chart for additional locations).

Unplanned Trips: These generally come in the form of bread and milk runs. However, they can frequently be for diapers, baby formula and, when the women are away, beer. Each trip is worth about 100 calories.

12 or 16 oz. Curls: This is a body building technique that most women are unwilling to undertake because it requires the lack of small children, morals and brain power to accomplish.

Yelling: They yell at the TV more than women do. Politics, sports, and the Hunting Channel give you more to yell about than the Ellen, Lifetime, and Oprah ever could (except at the gym, but there it's patently uncool).

Scotch: It's a replacement for protein shakes. When used to excess, it not only keeps the male from eating, but in severe cases performing all but the most basic bodily functions including reverse peristalsis which counts as -10 calories consumed.

Faster Metabolism: It is true, most men burn calories more quickly than women, particularly around the time the *Sports Illustrated* swimsuit issue is published.

Relating to Food: In general, women tend to be more emotional about food, whereas the majority of men are not willing to admit to having any emotions whatsoever.

Sex: When men think of romance, they are not thinking about food, going out to dinner and stopping for a night cap. This is a huge calorie saver.

Rules for Running

Even if you are not familiar with the runner's culture, it might be a good idea to take a moment and take a quick look at the rules — and when you are done, like stashing fine-money under "Free Parking" in *Monopoly*, you can make up some of your own. But, like the law of gravity, there are some rules for running that that are best-obeyed whether you run or not.

1: Don't run in the house. You should have learned this as a kid!

2: Get running shoes fitted at a running store. Wear them even if they are not cute, your feet, legs, knees, hips, and back will thank you for it.

3: Prevent injuries by strength-training. Nearly half of all runners are injured in any given year.

4: Prevent injuries by warming up and cooling down.

5: RICE (Rest, Ice, Compression and Elevation) is the most common treatment for soft tissue injuries.

6: Casts are the most common treatment for broken bones and sometimes face-palms.

7: Prevent injuries by stretching. 82 percent of runners will experience a running-related injury in their lifetime.

8: Have a training plan. What is the goal of your training? To run far? To run fast? To run a 5K? To get to the bar on time?

9: Have a flexible plan.

10: Lube the moving parts, starting with your crotch.

11: Celebrate your victories! Beer, bacon, selfies, and cake are a good start!

12: Don't increase mileage or intensity too much each week, use the 10% rule.

13: The best run is the one you don't skip.

14: The worst run is the one where you should have taken Imodium® and didn't.

15: Don't just run, strength-train and cross-train, too. Be a beast!

16: Eat some carbs and protein within 30 minutes after a run (lots of geeky scientific reasons, just do it!).

17: Run facing traffic. You'd hate to miss your last second on earth without knowing what hit you.

18: Don't run right after eating Thanksgiving dinner. Take a nap first.

19: Remember, you are not on a bike. If you try to coast, as soon as your legs stop, the forward inertia will dump you flat on your face (it's a Newton thing).

20: If your muscles are sore after a run, that's a good thing.

21: Get enough sleep. It's best, though, if it's not while you're running.

22: Replace your shoes every 300-500 miles, or when they stink so badly they could choke a skunk, whichever comes first.

23: Learn to run long, slow runs and fast, short ones. Which is better? It depends on how long you have until the cops find out what you did.

24: If you run at night, make yourself visible. Most drivers are not using night-vision goggles.

25: If you have any sharp pains during/after running, that's probably a good sign that you should take a few days off.

26: You should be able to talk in complete sentences while running, presuming that you can normally talk in complete sentences when you are not running.

27: A headwind always slows you down more than a tailwind speeds you up. It's hearsay, but it feels that way.

28: Running uphill slows you down more than running downhill speeds you up. Also hearsay.

29: Don't run with scissors (should have learned this when you were a kid, too). If you are reading this, you probably still have eyes. (Dr. Finch: Where would we be without our painful childhoods?)

30: Take rest days! If you are new, start with four rest days each week and work up slowly but always take one (have a training plan!).

31: It's faster to pretend you are a bear, than wait in line for the porta-potty during a race.

32: Bring toilet paper on long runs.

33: Make your move just before you crest a hill; there is always a downhill to follow.

34: Sign up for races even if you can't win.

35: Run at least eight miles a week.

36: Creeps, crazies, rattlesnakes, and rabid dogs are your best opportunity for a magic mile.

37: Carry an ID; you may have to convince the paramedic that you are much older than twenty-two.

38: If you can't run by a bubbling brook, bring water.

39: Let the race come to you.

40: The GPS watch is a tool, but sometimes it's not the right one for the job.

41: The biggest mistake a runner can make is misplacing their running shoes.

42: To reduce boredom, run your routes backwards and see if you can confuse your GPS.

43: Never run a race with brand new shoes, shirts, shorts, skorts, or slow music.

44: Wash stinky clothes with a little vinegar.

45: A little bit of caffeine might fix what bacon and running doesn't.

46: Even if you are the only one, always run with encouraging people!

47: Running must be fun.

48: Run your own race.

49: 10% Rule: Spending one tenth of your income on race fees.

50: You don't need to carry a gun; pepper spray is more than enough for the treadmill at the gym.

51: Relax!

52: Have fun!

The Day the Music Died

Daylight arrived along with the soft pitter-patter of rain on the motel deck. "Oh God help me, this is it," I thought, as I gave up the idea of falling back to sleep. My mind ran through a few desperate prayers and I felt a sense of peace.

But I still had to get up.

It was the day of the "Hyannis Half Marathon". When I registered less than a month before, I had visions of a cold but sunny day. I pictured myself running along the beach and across the bridge in the marsh — it was glorious in the center of my imagination. Well, that didn't happen. In fact, almost 2,000 wimps did not even show up for the race (see rules 13 and 35). At first the weather services forecasted a snow storm, and it was touch-and-go until 5:00 PM the night before as to whether there was even going to be a race at all. Then my weather application said there was a chance of light rain (cold, raw, biting rain).

The Start: My wife and youngest daughter dropped me off across the street and I made my way to the Conference Center to get a hot coffee and use the men's room. I fiddled with my equipment (my GPS, mp3 player, etc., lest we confuse just which equipment I needed to fiddle with), put on my headphones, figured out how to wear my smartphone under my new running raincoat, and restarted my phone so that I wouldn't have any issues with software. Then I left the dry warmth of the hotel and walked out into the rain, to the 10 minute pace corral, crossing a torrent of runoff on the way.

I tapped Endomondo to get it started, and pressed play on the music. Nothing — just *nothing!* There was no music and no time for fiddling with it any more; the "Star Spangled Banner" ended and the crowd of over 3,000 began to move towards the start line. There were so many runners that it took a full three minutes for them all to cross the timer grid.

Mile 1: It was more of a slow jog with lots of brightly-colored runners clogging Sea Street. I didn't really get warmed up as I customarily would, so the slow start was actually a good thing. I smiled to myself. My feet were still dry, and the rain so far, was light.

Yeah, the weather was horrible, and two thousand wimps who'd registered didn't even show up. It was in the 30s and it rained on and off the entire race. Four to five inch deep puddles dashed all hope of dry feet. Still, it was glorious.

Mile 2: Things began to loosen up and the pack started to spread out. Endomondo reported fourteen minutes to mile one. What? It is working, but there was still no music!

Mile 3: I reminded myself of what my friend Tom had said to me on Facebook: "Let the race come to you." We turned the corner and headed past the harbor toward the beach. A steady headwind blew rain into my face and I trudged on down the road, jumping the occasional puddle.

Mile 4: Running along the beach is where I met up with Team Joe. Joe was blind from diabetes. He had a fellow leading him with a lanyard, warning him of obstacles. There was still a fair amount of traffic, so we could keep up a conversation. We shared our survivor stories and then I picked up the pace and moved past them.

Mile 5:   Huge puddles covered the width of the road and we had to run on lawns to avoid them. Then the inevitable, too much water and vented running shoes. My toasty warm feet were now soaked and cold. Water squished out of the vent holes with every step, causing sea foam to form around the lace holes.

Mile 6:   The worst hill of the race took up most of mile six, where I encountered lots of walkers, of which I became one. I went through the water-stop where I grabbed a handful of refreshment. I had a quick cup of H2O and ate a raspberry energy-thingy.

Mile 7:   It was there that I started to doubt myself. God, it was windy, cold and even though the rain was light, it was relentless and had soaked through everything. A gust of wind blew my glasses off. I found a zippered pocket in my new raincoat, stuffed them safely inside and ran without them. Three kids, probably all under ten, were just so excited about the race they were high-fiving everyone — me too (it's great to have fans; they probably didn't even know that I was an action hero).

I had a brief thought, I was a heart attack survivor, and I am running a half marathon. How cool is that?!

Mile 8:   I hit the next water-stop to stretch and massage my sore knee. I drank a few sips of water, and on I ran on thinking about those three kids. It was surreal; like I wasn't even there — well, except that my knee was worse with the cold, damp wind.

Mile 9:   The right knee started feeling better, and a tailwind along with a slight downhill contributed to my fastest mile: 9:35.

In the middle of an intersection there was a guy clapping and yelling, "This is New England running at its best, come on let's pick it up!" I felt a little encouragement.

Mile 10:   Honestly, I was wishing it would just be over, but I was just too close to quit.

Mile 11:   Part of the route was on a state highway and they made us run two abreast. The shoulder of the road was 3 inches deep in runoff water, so I walked on the outside of the cones for a few hundred yards.

Mile 12:   I went into a trance of sorts, running through some of the Hyannis neighborhoods where I once lived. My arms were numb. I gave up dodging puddles and took the shortest route. A gal on the side of the road yelled a convincing "you've got this!" and gave me a high-five. It was emotional — I needed that just about then.

Mile 13: I asked one of the race marshals, "how much farther?"

"You are almost there!"

And then suddenly I heard music playing in the distance.

To The Finish: I rounded the bend and headed up the hill. Under a sea of umbrellas were my wife, her cousin and her husband, and my very wet, but very excited nine-year-old cheering me on. A couple of high-fives, as I cranked it up and raced across the timing strip passing six or seven runners in the last hundred yards.

The next few minutes were very personal and life changing.

It's hard to express how it feels to have been in the I.C.U. less than 2 years before, have run my first 5K eleven months before, and to have finished my first half-marathon. A sense of accomplishment that seemed only to be ever more satisfying as each of my goals were met after all the determination, hard work and training I'd invested, along with faith, prayer and the support and encouragement of my family and friends. No, it's really quite difficult to put it into words.

The Aftermath: A two-inch blister on my left foot, bleeding nipples (yes, I wore all the right stuff!), very sore quads, and an overwhelming sense of awe at what I have been able to accomplish in spite of the song that had played over and over telling me I would never be a runner, it was too far, I was too old, my knees would give out.

That song is dead.

CHAPTER FIFTEEN

You Can't Make This Up

Through the hard work of diet and exercise (coupled with not dying), life changed dramatically for me. Some unusual situations have presented themselves since my humble beginnings. Actually, my life has been a parade of unusual situations (enough for another book). Ever since I had lost my pants in the full-body scanner at airport security, I pay close attention to whether or not they fit (not normally a guy thing, but I believe I've evolved). I check to make sure that labels and hang tags are carefully removed, and that my underwear is clean in case I get in an accident while taking the trash can to the curb in the dark (see, I really did listen to my mom's advice).

Admittedly, changing so many questionable health habits has been a little tough on me. My friend (who will remain unnamed because he didn't buy a copy of my book…yet) said that you can't start the next chapter of your life if you keep rereading the last one. That's why, when we moved during the summer of 2013, I decided to get rid of all the clothes that no longer fit me. Now that I had lost the non-alcoholic beer belly, there was no going back. It took a few trips to the donation bin to haul it all out there; I chose the one in front of the big man's store to tap into some good karma; it was a spiritually-cleansing experience.

Making a pilgrimage to the classiest store I knew of, Targét (tar-jay), I purchased some new unmentionables. Buying underwear at Wal-Mart just doesn't make a man feel desirable, just utilitarian. I chose the package that had a model with ripped abs — more karma, I'd hoped. Another new chapter of life had begun!

One day, in my usual hurry to get going, I pulled on a new pair of blue ones. It's a favorite color of the Mrs. Then I headed out the door for a hot and humid five mile run. At mile two I had to stop because something was chaffing my right buttock about midway down. It was a piece of clear plastic tape from the packaging. Don't fret, no one was looking, and it wasn't done by a schoolyard — that's Julio's job anyway. After forty-five minutes on the road, I pushed open the front door to the house. As I stripped down to get in the shower, that's when I let out a little gasp. Upon closer inspection, all the moving parts were tinted blue as though they were oxygen-deprived (apparently that really neat blue color comes through copious amounts of dye in the manufacturing process).

That same summer I finished another long run. Stretching against the pillar by the front door, letting my heart rate settle down, I went inside. I walked into the laundry room and took off my stinky clothes, pitching them into the hamper (more evidence of my manly evolution). Then I decided to get a cool glass of water in the kitchen before getting into the shower. I had forgotten that our new kitchen was on the first floor with a window right next to the sidewalk. There I stood face-to-face with a neighbor who was standing there, plastic bag in hand, waiting for her black lab to do his business. My sweaty feet squeaked against the kitchen floor as I made an instantaneous about-face, running back to the bathroom in shame. In a flash, I thought, "oh, God, I hope she doesn't go to my church!"

Along the path to losing nearly eighty pounds, people started to notice that I was losing weight. I actually was a little upset that it was forty pounds before anyone actually acknowledged the change. Most of them were nice saying things like "You look great". Even though I know I had quite a bit more to lose, I would just say "thank you".

Another time, someone asked, "Wow, what happened to you?"

"I got my belly caught in a meat grinder changing my shirt in the kitchen. Fortunately I had pants on at the time." I smiled.

There are those that seemed a little insensitive to my plight, others were downright nosey. In life there are questions that are better off not asked. Everyone should have the common sense not to ask a woman how much they weigh or how old they are — and you never, ever ask "When is your due date?", unless her navel has a little hand waving hello. This is as important as the Golden Rule. Even a woman eventually learns not to ask her husband if they look fat in "this" dress (though it will always remain a go-to psychological weapon in their arsenal — married guys, you know of what I speak).

Whatever your body image might be, it's always good to be prepared for thoughtless questions.

A fellow that I knew pretty well from church decided that we were close enough that he would risk it all on this question: "How much did you weigh before?", he asked eyeing my waistline.

"My mom said it was eight pounds, four ounces." I smiled.

Snarky Comebacks to Inconsiderate Clods

Since I became thinner, I have also become a mind-reader. It comes in handy with kids who don't want to tell the truth, and knowing which face to use during a discussion on feelings with my wife after she says. "I don't need you to fix this, I just want you to listen." It is also handy to have a ready answer when family, friends and co-workers would like to you eat things that are no longer on your grocery list.

I hate it when "no thank you" doesn't work! There seems to be no shortage of inconsiderate clods who insist on offering you food, suggest the worst restaurants for lunch, pour one-thousand calorie drinks, and display plates of sweet, deadly treats.

So, for all of those awkward social situations you might find yourself in, here are some helpful responses (no extra charge, you've already paid for the book). You can re-gender any of them as your own circumstances may require:

You should have a beer.

No thanks, I am going skydiving at lunch and don't want to splatter on the roof of your wife's mini-van/husband's BMW, it might scare the hell out of the kids, and you'll never get the stains out of the upholstery.

Have another piece of cake.

So, I can look like you?

Let's stop at McDonald's.

You are what you eat, and I am not interested in being fat, cheap or passed out a window.

You should have some (Name of some food item that everyone knows causes instantaneous stroke).

I am allergic to sugar, fat and sodium; it causes me to go into violent, foaming convulsions just before I go into shock — but thanks for asking.

Let's go to KFC.

I heard someone got a fried mouse there — pretty gross, right? At least he was coated in extra-crispy batter first.

Have a piece of pizza.

I just saw (the name of the person most disliked in the office) sneeze on it. It's hard to tell with the broccoli, I know.

How about a Margarita?

No thanks; I was looking for a José/Juanita about my age with ripped abs.

Try some banana nut bread.

I can't, I am fasting for my colonoscopy. Actually, I need to run…

You are a vegetarian?

Yes, the only animals I eat are crackers. But seriously, I don't eat anything with a face. That's why I immediately decapitate everything I kill.

It's good for you.

Let's see (picking up the package and reading the panel of ingredients) — Bleached Flour, Corn Syrup, Sugar, High Fructose

Corn Syrup, Hydrogenated Vegetable and Animal Shortening, Dextrose, Modified Corn Starch, Glucose, Leavenings (Sodium Acid Pyrophosphate, Baking Soda, Monocalcium Phosphate), Sweet Dairy Whey, Soy Protein Isolate, Calcium and Sodium Caseinate, Salt, Mono and Diglycerides, Polysorbate 60, Soy Lecithin, Soy Flour, Cornstarch, Cellulose Gum, Sodium Stea-roylLactylate, Sorbic Acid (to Retain Freshness), Yellow 5, and Red 40 — yummy!

Stop, Drop and Roll

The gym is the stage for a plethora of strange happenings and paranormal (or just abnormal) human behavior. It seems that one remarkable occurrence eclipses the next; never a dull moment for people-watchers.

One cold afternoon as the wind drifted the snow outside, three dozen of us lined up on our treadmills beneath four large flat screen TVs. It was like a scene out of *Clockwork Orange*. *Ellen*, Olivia from *Law and Order*, Pat Summerall, and CNN's Wolf Blitzer lip synched "Paranoid" by Black Sabbath in my headphones as the miles wore on. I was enjoying my back row view as I thought about finally graduating from the C25K program. I was little bit proud of myself as I ran along at 6.2 miles per hour. I dreamed of one day pushing it to the maximum of twelve!

The tread hummed along circulating on unseen rollers beneath my feet. As the music played, I tried my best to discreetly pass a little gas, and headed to the two-mile mark. With so many people in that small space, who would know from whence it might have come? A woman came and took the treadmill next to mine. She fiddled with her water bottle and car keys. From the corner of my eye I saw her pushing every button but the green one to start the machine. Gym rules are strange, they don't allow talking, especial-ly to members with headphones on, of which I was one. Then she started to bang on the control panel loudly enough where I could tell she was becoming frustrated. Because of the no talking rule, I pretended not to notice. Furiously pushing buttons and banging on the machine, but not one of the sheeple came to her aid. Finally I realized that it was my mission in life to hit the quick start button for her. Popping out my right headphone, I asked, "Do you need some help?"

"Do I look like I know what I am doing?" she snapped.

Oh my God, this is a trick question for which there is no right answer. Instead of talking, I reached over and pushed the green button. At that very moment I stepped on the side rail of my treadmill, my headphone cord wrapped itself around the handrail. Off the end of the spinning deck I went at 6.2 miles per hour, my body slamming the wall behind me. My glasses flew onto the belt, firing them back at mach ten, impaling my left shoulder. The woman turned to see what happened as I was writhing on the floor in pain. As she turned, she too lost her footing. Like the game "Mousetrap", her stupid water bottle came crashing down, dislodging the cover and creating a momentary lawn sprinkler as the tread continued to spin.

The runner on the other side of me calmly switched off both treadmills, grabbing her soggy *People* magazine and left in a huff. I too decided that it was best to leave. As the silent TVs flashed above the scene like the many marquis of Times Square at night, I put my headphone back in to make sure no one talked to me, and slipped out the back exit.

Annoying Habits of the Gym Culture

There are those that think of the gym as a large bathroom, some a bedroom, and worse, others a changing room. And most annoying of all, a phone booth if you are   old enough to know that one of those is.

Here is a list of some of the most annoying habits of gym culture.

Cell-phones: It is nice that it is much more common for people to do something else besides talk on their cell-phone, especially one with bad reception. The problem now is not just the chatter, but the fact is that, in order to fart and chew bubble gum, they have to sit on a weight machine until they comment on a Facebook post or text LOL to a wrong number.

Overly revealing outfits: Maybe it's just me, but it seems like there is a lot of unnecessary skin. I don't mind it on your face, or your arms, not even your legs. But for crying out loud, wear a shirt, sir!

Dropping Weights: If you can't lift them, don't use them, and if you can lift them, it doesn't make you any more macho or impress the lady in the French-cut leotard by dropping them to the floor from over your head when you're done with your set, you just confirm to everyone that you're the egomaniacal Neanderthal we all thought you were when you came in.

Odor: I am not sure which is worse, body odor, or excessive perfume to cover up the body odor. Please take a quick shower if you need to, the locker room is right over there!

Yoga Mats: If I can smell what went on using that thing, wash it!

Pooling Sweat: I don't care if it is genetics, please wipe the machine, removing your every single strand of D.N.A. Take a tip from Ford Prefect: always know where your towel is.

Weights: Didn't your mother ever tell you, if you took it out, put it away? Well, gentleman, this rule applies to the gym, not just the bathroom.

Staring: See, overly revealing outfits for starters. If you don't want to be looked at, I suppose you could dress like it, or stay home. It is doubtful the offenders are reading a book like this.

Grunting: It's not appreciated anywhere other humans are present.

Make Up: I am not sure why anyone cares about this. It makes your face lift look better.

Sauna Etiquette: No one likes a guy who pretends he's not naked when he is. I think this is a Finnish trait, but I am not sure.

Sunset on the Serengeti

The evening sun inched closer to the horizon, its warm glow shown though the plate glass windows as it cast a gentle shadow on the woman using the treadmill in front of me. She was new to the herd. I could tell by the fact she had left the garment tags on her new velour sweat suit. It is a rite of passage.

The liquid orange glow, as beautiful as the African plains themselves, gave a peaceful and surreal feeling to the cardio room — a cozy sense of belonging and security. Experienced runners and joggers surrounded the newborn foal as her hang tags bounced from cheek to cheek, dancing in the shimmer of polyester. Suddenly, and without warning, the treadmill like a lion on the prowl, swallowed one of her legs whole as she went down, as though she had been punched by a prize fighter. For some reason unbeknownst to everyone watching in horror, except for God himself, she did not go completely off the treadmill. The wild belt attacked the polyester pile, and piping with the fury of a cheetah on a wildebeest. A plume of purple smoke rose over the savanna as a torrent of fuzz poured off the machine — it was like standing in front of a wood chipper. Someone reached over and hit the emergency kill switch. The attendants came running, and she was whisked away faster than a sex offender on a rerun of *Law and Order, SVU*. A tense calm fell over the nervous herd. Who would be next, we wondered, as the warm glow of the setting sun glowed across the survivors down in Africa.

Shaming is Bad

There never seems to be an end to those that have a hard time accepting that running a marathon, losing weight, and a host of other things require some hard work, self discipline and grace from the heavenlies. Why else would they say, "I was on a diet and gained it all back". I'll be the first to admit, I have made a lot of mistakes, and given the opportunity to overeat, I have fallen. Through those times, I learned this: Once you learn to quit, it becomes a habit. Quitting can't be an option; in fact it shouldn't even be a choice, your brain should never go there.

Shamers (bad people) have many different reasons to minimize the accomplishments of those that make progress. It is not just in weight loss, or miles run, but it can happen in sports, at work, and church and even at home. Whether it is jealousy caused by the lack of self-confidence, their own poor self image, insecurity, sibling rivalry, the fear of someone else's awesomeness or sheer stupidity — don't expect everyone to be happy about your success.

How do you mange to be around people who say things like: "Haven't you lost enough?", " Why do you run?", "Do you need some money for food?", "You look anorexic", or "I liked you better before". I suggest that, unless you are talking to another runner, you don't brag about the miles which you run (the average American doesn't even know that a marathon is 26.2 miles, they think those stickers on the backs of cars denote the mileage they get). Instead, talk about how much you can have for dessert, and then have two servings. Another good idea is to stage an event in which your training becomes so important, they will become believers. For example, renting a live tiger and letting it loose in the backyard. Invite your favorite shamers over for a pool-side margarita. As the tiger (or lion, or cheetah, or panther depending which is in season) rounds the corner by the lawn shed, scream! Then take off running down the block. Everyone knows that the slowest runner is always dinner in a situation like that. Then return just in time to say "that's why" or "just kidding", whichever fits. If you become a heavy lifter, or an Ironman, you could make a beer run on your bicycle to the package store that is fifty miles away. Beer usually shuts people up if it's free. Or you could have the car "purposely" break down 26.2 miles from the nearest help. It's best to do it in an area that is notorious for street gang violence, drug dealers and muggers, with no cell coverage. Then run for help, becoming the savior of your favorite shamer. If these seem too impractical, any situation where the average person would poop their Fruit of the Looms, is a good opportunity to show off a little.

No matter what, you'll be hard pressed to find a human on "fitness fantasy land"who wouldn't like to burn 20,640 calories for doing 480 minutes of absolutely nothing each day. The truth is that if you weighed about 2,200 pounds (100 kilos), you might be able to.

CHAPTER SIXTEEN

The Change of Life

~~Call me Ishmael.~~
~~In a hole in the ground there lived a Hobbit.~~
~~All this happened, more or less.~~
~~Life is difficult.~~
~~A man is as he thinketh.~~
~~Whether I shall turn out to be the hero of my own life, or whether that station will be held by anybody else, these pages must show.~~
~~All children except one grow up.~~

Life is a constantly-changing journey — you can count on it. Somehow it is easy to be deceived that *where* we are in life will stay the same. It's a proven fact that the human heart is programmed in such a fashion, never to realize the vapor that their very existence really is. Most of mankind would rather be somewhere else in life than where they are right now — unless, of course, you're reading this while on vacation in some idyllic locale. It's especially true if you are reading this in the bathroom atop your hairy knees. Somehow we have been divinely wired to believe that "old" is always twenty years older than we are at any given moment in our lives. As a kindergartner, we believed that old was twenty-five. At age thirty, it was fifty, and at fifty it's supposed to be that seventy is *old*. At seventy, who knows? I haven't gotten there yet, maybe one hundred? Maybe I'll write another book about it when I make it that far…Lord willing.

In the movie *City Slickers*, Billy Crystal captures the essence of this phenomenon perfectly as he speaks to his son's grade school class…

"Value this time in your life, kids. This is the time in your life when you have choices. It goes by so fast. When you are a teenager, you think that you can do anything, and you do. Your twenties are a blur. In your thirties you make a little money, raise a family, and wonder, 'What happened to my twenties?' In your forties, you grow a potbelly and another chin. The music starts to get too loud, and one of your old girlfriends becomes a grandmother. In your fifties, you have a minor surgery — you call it a 'procedure'. In your sixties, you have a major surgery and the music is still loud, but that doesn't matter because you can no longer hear it. In your seventies, you and the wife move to Florida, and you start having dinner at 2 in the afternoon, lunch at 10 in the morning, and breakfast the night before. You spend most of your time wandering around malls looking for the ultimate low-fat yogurt and muttering, 'How come the kids don't call'? In your eighties you have a major stroke and end up babbling to a Jamaican nurse whom your wife can't stand, but who you end up calling 'Momma'."

The real question is this: When, in that descending time line, does one decide to get healthy and fit? If you are like me, you'll wait until you are in an I.C.U. with a cannula in your nose, hallucinating from the effects of Fentanyl, and checking to see if the pain in your crotch is from the family jewels having dropped off in the process — or not.

Being motivated, inspired, or taking control — whatever you want to call the D.N.A. of deciding to be healthier, it's a decision only you can make. Like any spiritual endeavor, it takes time, effort, knowledge, and a measure of grace. I can't supply the time, the effort, or the grace, however, I do have a little bit of friendly advice that is derived from my own pathetic life experiences.

The easiest way to get control of the metabolic process is to find out what your body actually needs in terms of fuel to simply exist on a day-to-day basis. How much food and drink is enough (how many calories per day)? That is the question. If you have the inkling to knock off a few pounds, then the total daily amount of calories your body needs to function, plus those burned during exercise, must be less than what you consume by eating. This creates a deficit, which causes the body to use energy already stored in your body — like a hibernating bear. What is this magic number? It's an *estimate* based on a mathematical formula, which uses a number of variables including height, weight, and age. Then it makes liberal use of a couple of fudge factors, and — voila! — you have something called "Total Daily Energy Expenditure"or T.D.E.E. Scientific terms make you sound like an expert, but to keep it simple, all you need to do is a web search for "weight loss calculator" and you'll find a gajillion sites with them. You'll notice too, that if you shop around for the best T.D.E.E., not every calculator agrees. Why? The entire caloric measuring system is based on a process which can have a number of errors and unpredictable variables. It is bit like the Environmental Protection Agency's (E.P.A.) "estimated fuel mileage" posted on the window sticker of a new car. Because no two drivers are exactly alike, traffic and weather conditions vary, as well as the condition and tuning of the individual car, the actual mileage is not completely predictable. Therefore, calories are not a "rule", they're more of a guideline! I would add, though, that calories are a very useful guide, but still a guide nevertheless.

Whatever method you use to gain insight into you caloric intake and output, it is best to use the same method all the time. If your T.D.E.E. is off by five or even ten percent, you can adjust your meals or exercise accordingly. The only way to really know what is going on with your body is metabolic testing. Of course, the method used to figure out difference in calories between a ten ounce steak and a double chocolate chip cookie has its own mystical properties. The Scientific American website had this to say: "According to the National Data Lab (NDL), most of the calorie values in the U.S.D.A. and industry food tables are based on indirect calorie estimations made using the so-called Atwater system." I have no idea who Atwater was (or is), and how he came up with this system of his. To me, it's just more proof of the voodoo/mojo science of caloric estimation.

I would like to reiterate, calories are estimates and best used as a guide! If your estimates are correct, and you have calculated your caloric deficit using one of the many websites, you should start losing weight. It would be nice if this was a perfect system, but it's not, which can be frustrating. Although I haven't looked to see if there is a specific study out there, here are a couple of things that I have noticed. The more you have to lose, the faster it seems to come off. For some it's tough to get the process started, which is especially true when you begin exercising at the same time. One trainer told me that the body can retain as many as ten pounds of water in order to manage the muscle repair of a beginner. The body eventually adapts to a regular workout routine and all of sudden there can be a week when the weight drops significantly as it finally makes that adjustment all at once. The other problem is that, as muscle is being formed and fat is being consumed, the readings on your scale may not change, even though your body has become leaner. The tape measure can be your friend as the muscle and fat reconfigure into the new you. Age, of course, is a big factor in the ability of the human body to respond to these changes.

Change is a process, which, as you incorporate some of the suggestions in this book, should slowly make you healthier and fitter. I can't guarantee it, but these have been my experiences and observations, so it's probably true!

Personal Success

Your personal success is never a given (and not guaranteed by the author, nor the contributors to this book), but here are a few more tips for the journey:

Schedule your workouts like you would a gynecology appointment (or guys, your urologist). You may not want to go, but you know you need to take thirty minutes three times a week to move as much and as fast as you can.

Log all your food, and as suggested previously, count calories — all of them. Then log your exercise calories (how much you've burned). Google "easy math" if you need a little more help in this area. There are a host of weight loss and fitness apps, as well as websites where you can manage all of this. Some of the apps even allow you to scan barcodes from food packages to keep track, but it still requires discipline.

When you log, like a checkbook register or balance sheet, you make additional deposits to your calorie account by exercising. By comparison, they will be smaller than your regular daily "burn". Eating back your exercise calories is recommended, but due to the not-entirely-reliable estimation process, it might not work, so try *not* eating them! As you already know, calorie counting is not a perfect science, but it is the best guide to understanding your personal metabolism.

Weigh your food portions. I suspect you didn't get to where you are now by being able to accurately estimate the weight of a rib eye steak at thirty paces! This is especially true with higher calorie foods such as desserts, nuts, peanut butter, chips, meat, fish, and poultry. If you get three teaspoons of peanut butter instead of two, that can add about 100 calories to your day.

Get rid of all the food in the house that does not support your new lifestyle. These don't just have to be foods that make you fat, but they could be ones that increase your risk of diabetes, heart disease, and cancer. Depending on how much you need to throw out, this may be quite a project, so you may log your cabinet-clean-up as "cardio exercise"!

Take "before" pictures now. If you are serious about this, take some ugly "fat" pics (maybe even a few "selfies" in the buff)! Fifty pounds from now, you'll be glad you did. I look back at the photos that you've seen in this book, and just smile. When you see the one of me on my bio page and see the "after" image, you can see how inspiring those "before" shots can be. That's why I shared them with you.

Use the tape measure often, and the scale sparingly. Your weight will fluctuate as much as five pounds per day. The sign of healthy weight loss is lower body fat percentages (not lower body fat, like when your butt jiggles).

Knowing what you are going to eat as far in advance as possible is the key to long-term success. A seven-day plan can help you navigate things at home. A weekly meal plan, lunches made and frozen before the work week, and planning for holidays and parties is essential.

Visit your favorite restaurant sites now and make a list of suitable meals at each of them. You really can get out of most places with a 400 to 600 calorie meal if you plan for it (ordering impulsively as you scan the menu while trying to maintain a conversation with your significant other can spell caloric Armageddon — it's best to have a plan to avoid disaster).

Stop making excuses for overeating. Maybe you should let the dog eat what's in the doggie bag! It's your life, make the most of it. At the same time, if you fall off the wagon, don't think that you've failed and it's hopeless — just climb back on and put it in your past. Vigilance is the key to staying on track, but we're all human so don't beat yourself up about it.

Stop paying with pennies! It makes people mad who are waiting in line behind you!

Now I Am a Fitness Nazi

My wife and I had a parent conference with my daughter Charlotte's teacher; at the time, she was an energetic nearly nine-year-old. During the meeting, our worst fears were confirmed — she is just like her father. After recovering from her shock, my wife and I got to thinking after the meeting, that she probably needs some help focusing on her diet and fitness. Charlotte is a super-fussy eater and skinny as a rail, but it is still good to invest in a balanced diet and some exercise, which will be a good lifestyle foundation for her as she goes through the phases of life that Billy Crystal so eloquently described (of course, at nine years old, we never believe any of that stuff; at fifty, we wonder why).

With her help, I created a sports calendar for her to choose three sports activities each week to do with me for fifty minutes (thirty for cardio, and twenty for whining about not doing it). We were about a week into it and she enjoyed choosing from ice hockey, biking, tennis, basketball, soccer, running, anything else she thought she would like. Her response when asked to choose some activities? "You are not the boss of me!"

"I thought this was going to be fun", I replied. She got the vibe, and started to check off a few things.

Our first week was a complete success. It was father-daughter time, and allowed me to do a little cross training. She played ice hockey alone, spent twenty minutes kicking the soccer ball around, and thirty minutes passing and dribbling the basketball. The high point of her routine with dad was her first outing on rollerblades. It went something like this.

"Do you need help with your equipment, kiddo?"

(Pre-adolescent eye-roll) "I'll let you know." (Time lapse of 11 seconds.) "Can you help me with my wrist guards?"

"You don't know where your wrists are?" I asked.

"Please!" she whined.

I smiled, "why certainly, let me see your left hand."

She smiled a little. "Thanks, Dad!" Then she asked, "How are we going to get *up* the hill?"

"Skate!" I replied.

"That's nuts!" she exclaimed. "And Dad, put on your helmet. You know how you are."

"How am I?" I asked.

"Well Mommy says... ahh nothing." She said, as she reached to steady herself on all eight wheels.

Off we went stepping up over the curb onto the walkway at the park. We skated up the gradual hill and around the beautiful fall lawns and gardens of the 9/11 Memorial.

"I am doing good, right Dad?" She asked as her self-confidence began to rise.

"Yes better than your mom! — Perfect — excellent!" I replied with a smile.

It was awesome, father and daughter hand-in-hand

October 7, 2013

Charlotte had her first day on roller-blades. I am glad she is taking time to get some exercise and spend some quality father-daughter time with me. It was a lot of fun with a few exciting moments.

Photo by: David Johndrow

rollerblading in the splendor of a New England fall. Each lap around the park, Charlotte loosened up a little more. I could tell she was really enjoying it. Then without warning, on the last half mile of our five-mile skate, she went down. All I could hear was her plastic guards scraping along the pavement. And then I realized we were connected in a death grip.

Spinning around on the wet leaves was the last thought I had before: Stop, drop, and roll!

Too late.

Well, at least I wasn't on fire. The pain jumped from one skinned joint to another, and I lay on my back in the grass.

She got to her feet, "Dad, quit playing, you're alright. — Umm, aren't you?"

And I was worried about *her!*

I got back up on my skates and we made our way to the car to assess my injuries; now you know why they call it asphalt.

"You don't even need a Band-Aid for that", she said looking at my skinned knee. "But I am really sorry, Dad."

"I'll be fine," I said.

"I'll tell Mommy how brave you were. You didn't even cry."

"Thank you, Pumpkin."

All this fitness and healthy eating is dangerous. I just thank God her mother is handling the food!

Monday, Bloody Monday

I woke up, it was my short-run day, an easy five or six miles. I should have been excited about the perfect spring weather, the sunshine, two cups of my favorite coffee, nature making its move before the run, and thinking about my next race. Instead, as I got dressed, I watched the news, the horror, the images of the sidewalk I have been on dozens of times, and the Boston Marathon finish line strewn with bomb blast debris.

The day before had started out perfectly. My wife and our 9-year-old got up and walked the mile down to the race route nearby where we lived outside of Boston, near the 10K checkpoint (mile 6.1 of 26.2). There we cheered and clapped for thousands of runners as we waited to high-five our friends who had entered the race, and would be running past.

Charlotte sat on my shoulders and my wife stood by my side. "What color is Tommy wearing?" she asked.

"He's wearing a red shirt with white lettering and dark blue shorts, I saw him in the picture he posted on Facebook. And the ladies are wearing purple. And Tom is wearing a dark blue running club tank-top."

My cell phone buzzed with a text message. Lori, a seasoned marathoner, was killing it, forty-four minutes to the 10K checkpoint. She drifted over close to the ropes for a quick high-five.

Ten minutes later, the next buzz and Tommy showed up with a huge grin. "Fifty-five minutes," I shouted and high-fived him as he went by. It was his first Boston Marathon.

Then Tom came through. "One hour buddy, you are on pace for a personal best!" Another high-five, and off he ran. Tom and I had been friends for many years, and had run a couple of shorter races together.

We waited another five minutes or so, and Kelly shouted from the middle of the road, "hey David!"

"Good luck!" I yelled back as I waved.

Amidst the throngs of cheering Bostonians, the balloons, and the clanging cowbells, we made our way to a small diner, with a view of the race route, for lunch. We ordered sandwiches to the backdrop of muted cheers, and a parade of color as we sat watching with continued excitement.

All the way home we talked about the crazy costumes, funny t-shirts, and how fun it was to see our friends among 23,000 others, not including the hundreds of "bandits" running without numbers. If I didn't have to work, I would have been one of them.

Back home sitting at my desk, I posted the checkpoint times of my friends to Facebook as they made the 20K and 30K checkpoints and texted me. I got my last text at 1:47 pm. Tommy had made the 30K checkpoint at 3:04:04. The others had past it a few minutes earlier.

I was expecting to get more updates around 2:47 pm. Lori had already finished in three hours and thirty minutes. The others were all on pace for a finish in about four hours.

Nothing.

I was checking the BAA website, and no finish times were recorded. The website must be overloaded, I thought. Then I noticed someone posted something on My Fitness Pal about bombs going off at the Boston Marathon finish line. I Googled it, and got the first news stories and viewed a terrifying photo. I scanned it looking for signs of my friends. I saw that Lori had "liked" a Facebook posting, so I messaged her to see if Tommy was alright.

No answer.

I texted the guys on my phone, and left posts on their Facebook pages: "Just let me know you are OK."

No answer.

At 3:42 pm I heard that Tommy was OK. Later, I heard that the purple team was all accounted for. Thank God. It took until early evening until Tom was able to return my text. He was safe in his Boston hotel.

For those of you who run, you know what the camaraderie between those in the sport can be. These are my friends. We speak the same language, we run together, we encourage one another, and we support each others' fund-raising efforts. Occasionally we see each other at other functions, too.

How could I process all this?

That day I was angry, tearful, and thankful all at once, and as I first wrote this chapter as an entry on my blog site, I was deter-

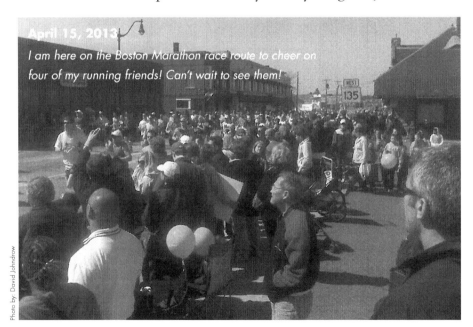

April 15, 2013
I am here on the Boston Marathon race route to cheer on four of my running friends! Can't wait to see them!

Photo by: David Johndrow

mined. I dedicated my morning run that next day to thinking and praying for those three race fans that died as a result of the evil that a very small group of humans seemed relentless to perpetrate on others.

Because I am an American, a Christian, a runner, a husband, a father, and the protector of my family, my heart goes out to those who lost loved ones, those who have lost limbs, to those who are scared, and to those who just freakin' care about their fellow man, and are saddened by this act of violence. As a runner, I also have a response. I am going to run. The first chance I get, I am going to run in downtown Boston. I am going to remember, and I am going to pray. I am going to be sad for those who worked so hard, only to be robbed of the victory of finishing the greatest race on earth: The Boston Marathon.

In the days that followed, we came to know more about the lives lost, and even more about the plot to kill Americans. The tributes during Boston sporting events were touching, tearful — amazing! The rallying cry of "Boston Strong" began to be heard from the midst of the mourning, and angst as the authorities hunted for those responsible for the attack. The memorial in downtown grew rapidly along with the anger, and the resolve to take our lives back. There were a couple of bright spots as we watched the stories of survivors and those that came to their aid. As a city, Boston began the recovery.

Stephen Colbert did a funny and touching sketch on his show. Here is a transcript:

"Tonight — look, before we begin, I just want to take a moment to talk about the attack in Boston yesterday. Obviously, our thoughts and our prayers are with everybody there. And as the president said, we don't know who did this, but they will be found, and they will be brought to justice. But whoever did this obviously did not know s#*%t about the people of Boston. Because nothing these terrorists do is going to shake them. For Pete's sake, Boston was founded by the Pilgrims — a people so tough they had to buckle their goddamn hats on. It is the cradle of the American Revolution. A city that withstood an 86-year losing streak. A city that made it through the Big Dig, a construction project that backed up traffic for 16 years — I mean, there are commuters just getting home now. Even their bands are tough. It's the hometown of Aerosmith, who are, in their fifth decade, still going strong. Even Steven Tyler looks fantastic, for a 73-year-old woman.

But here is what these cowards really don't get. They attacked the Boston Marathon. An event celebrating people who run 26 miles on their day off until their nipples are raw, for fun. And they have been holding it in Boston since 1897. And do you know how tough you have to be to run in a whalebone corset? And when those bombs went off, there were runners who, after finishing a marathon, kept running for another two miles to the hospital to donate blood.

So here's what I know. These maniacs may have tried to make life bad for the people of Boston, but all they can ever do is show just how good those people are."

It still makes me want to run, or pray, or hug my kids, or call a friend, or do something nice for someone.

CHAPTER SEVENTEEN

Follow Your Dreams, They Know the Way

Like so many humans, I have had dreams. My mind is busy with creative thoughts — thoughts about my family, my career, my art, and my health. There is a deeper layer which transcends my spirit, which somehow mysteriously commingles with the Spirit of God. The deepest desires of the human heart rarely surface in *speakable* words, and more rarely become a reality.

The difference between impossible and possible often lies in the heart of the one facing the challenge.

Standing at the starting line of the "Cape Cod Marathon", I faced the most daunting experience of my lifetime. My adrenaline-fueled heart raced with anticipation as I waited for the starting cannon of my first full marathon. I have to confess, I didn't even feel that anxious on August fourth, 1982, when I joined the Army, and was sworn in. Knowing that I would be going to get on a bus and arrive for basic training in the sweltering Alabama summer was more predictable than that moment on the starting line.

Marathons are often on peoples' bucket lists — it's something to experience. For me, the Cape Cod Marathon was not just a test of my physical and mental toughness; it was the proving ground of my faith. All the encouragement I had received from friends and cyber-friends eventually outweighed my own doubts. The dream and the possibility of success met in the middle of Main Street, in front of the Bank of America building. The culmination of which was to risk it all and travel 26.2 miles, running through the land first discovered by the Pilgrims who, I was reminded, were so tough, they had to buckle their hats to their heads.

Since I first witnessed the Boston Marathon, I have held on to a dream, a dream to finish a full marathon. It was the ultimate realization of the dream I had, lying like a flounder in a hospital bed, and that I worked up to by accomplishing one small goal at a time, each a little bigger than the one before. The first was to just show up and finish, eventually conquering a 5K race and a half-marathon, fighting the pain, the elements, and my own doubts about myself.

I fantasized running this marathon in four hours or less (the runner clock thing!), but deep down, I knew that wouldn't be possible for me. I had to lower my standards due to my physical limitations, but I never lost sight of that goal. Somewhere, out on that horizon, out beyond the neon lights, I know there must be something better, but there's nowhere else in sight (thanks to the Eagles for stealing my thoughts for their hit song, "In the City") — I knew there was a finish line, a finisher's medal, and a race certificate with my name on it — but deeper, there awaited the answer to a prayer.

The conflict over whether to run the marathon at all, or just put it off again, raged within me. And not solely because I lacked confidence in my ability, but another health concern surfaced at my last physical. The blood test for prostate cancer, although not very accurate, came back in the danger zone. The doctor said that I needed to schedule a biopsy; I told them I'd have to let them know when I would be ready for that. The wheels of negativity began to move like that big wheel on the desert island on *Lost*.

More fear of the unknown.

Add to that, a lay off at work, and all I felt like doing was sitting in the office chair zoning out on social media and browsing bacon recipes.

I finally committed to registering for the Cape Cod Marathon after a woman named Cherie Frank commented on a Facebook Group post, "David, I ran a marathon while I was having chemo treatments. I decided that it was six hours of my life which I could control." I was more convinced than I had ever been. As I clicked the "submit" button on the registration form, I told myself that I could still back out.

I had doubted my ability to run or even walk 26.2 miles for a very long time. Of course I trained, most of which was in the heat and humidity of the New England summer. As the long miles wore on, there always came a point in every run in which my heart rate skipped up to near the maximum, trying to provide oxygen to fuel the clamor of its muscles. The confidence builders, the long slow training runs were all virtually disastrous, ending in more walking than running.

Two days after registering, I ran a 5K race near home with my run bud, Scott. He is younger, and has more experience than I do for sure. Did I also mention that he is faster, a lot faster than I am! We met up at the starting line. Our last race, he ran with me to support me. This one he was running to win. He ran it and took sixth place overall, and second in his age group. To my shock, I also took second in my age group. True runner happiness is having a run bud that will never be in your age group. I have one.

October 20, 2013
My run bud Scott and me posing for pictures at the Douglas Family 5K the week before my first full marathon. We were both second place finishers in our respective age groups. Happiness is having a run bud that will never be in your age group!

Photo by: Lisa Motyka

As the days drew closer and my training tapered to nearly none, I became increasingly anxious. It was hard to sit still, and it was even harder *not* to go out for a ten-mile run on a glorious fall day. The last couple of runs were only two miles each, hardly enough mileage to lace up for. Running slow and easy when you are mentally ready for a race seems crazy, however, that is how you conserve every last ounce of energy for marathon — I'd hoped, anyway.

As a first-timer, I had doubts about myself, and then I had doubts about my training. The more experienced runners reminded me to just trust the plan. I had to put those horrid long runs out of my mind. They said, while I was asleep, my body was adapting (I couldn't tell if that was true or not because while that was supposedly happening, I was, of course, asleep).

I read that a runner should have a strategy for a road race, even if it is a relatively short one. The rule of thumb is to start out slow so you have something left at the end. Having a strategy made me think about those training runs where I had to take long walk breaks because I didn't have anything left in the tank. It's known as "hitting the wall", and I wanted to avoid it.

I studied the course through time-lapse videos posted online. My new plan was to take walk breaks right from the start and, depending on what I have left at the end of the race, run what I could. There were a couple of steep hills at miles nine and twelve, which I planned to walk up. In fact from mile nine until twenty-one are rolling hills. I did smile when I thought of my friend David Salvas saying, "I just hope there is a clock at the finish line after 26.2 miles, and not a calendar!"

To fight off the nerves twenty-four hours before, I scheduled my day so that it would have structure without being too intense. I need time to think. I guess it's like a race, I need to just take it slow knowing that there is enough time to eat, hydrate, pack my clothes and running gear, and drive two hours to my friend's home on Cape Cod. I needed to arrive in time to pick up my race bib at the expo. On race morning, I just wanted to think about racing and nothing else.

My day consisted of making sure that I drank fourteen cups of water, ate three bananas, and consumed a good balance of carbohydrates, protein, and bacon. I packed for my excursion using my anti-ADD list. The motorcycle? I serviced that the day before, so it wasn't not on my list of things to worry about. I just wanted to be standing at the starting line. I was ready!

I hugged and kissed my family goodbye and fired up the motorcycle. I wished that they were able to come, but standing at the finish line for all those hours is boring, and a Honda 1100cc is not exactly a family car.

As I headed southeast, I ran through a list of things I knew I had brought, and was hoping that I didn't forget anything. Because I have a motorcycle, I've learned to travel light. That means that I don't bring the customary two-of-everything. With my responsibilities behind me, I turned on to the interstate and poured on the throttle, cruising along in the midday sun.

The rush of the wind and the drone of the motor put me in a trance. I pictured myself running the Sippowisset Hills and rounding the corner by Woods Hole Lighthouse. It's one of the most photographed lighthouses in the United States. I visualized going easy on the flat miles early on, walking up the big hills, and then racing down the back sides. I thought about what it would be like to run four or five hours. I dreaded the possibility of having to take six hours to reach the finish line.

Soon enough I was at the rotary ("roundabout" for you foreigners and Vermonters), passing the restaurant where my wife and I had our first date. I stopped in the parking lot to check in with Facebook (not exactly Facebook foreplay). I sent a text to my friend to let him know I was getting close to his home, and then motored back onto Route Six.

There were three reasons I chose the Cape Cod Marathon. The first was that it was in a region of my state that I like to call home, having lived there for twenty-one years. The second reason was that it was a week later than the one I had originally planned, which gave me more time to procrastinate. My personal philosophy is "never do today what you can put off until tomorrow, and never put off until tomorrow what you can avoid altogether" — my waning confidence had me considering pushing it ever father out in the calendar. The third reason is more of an excuse; I had previously run the "Crawlin' Crab Half Marathon" in Hampton, Virginia. The course was very flat and one would be inclined to think that it would be the perfect course for going fast. As it turned out, it was my slowest half marathon of the three that I had run so far. Reason number three was rolling hills. Little did I know just how rolling they would be!

There is a lot more to running a marathon than running. It's easy to fantasize about bounding across the finish line. The reality is that even though I started training five months before the race, logging 192 miles in the month of August alone, I still had to go the distance in one day without any significant rest during the event. There were no TV time-outs, no half times, no shift changes or player substitutions — it would be foot to pavement continuously for over five solid hours. Nearly 50,000 steps!

Marathoning has other challenges: chafing, sunburn, blisters, hydration, fueling on the run and electrolyte balance. It was all new to me at this distance. Anyone can run a few miles in a t-shirt without chaffing, but getting through 26.2 miles is a different story. I ran three half marathons and had bloody nipples by the end of two of them. I had another half marathon where I didn't get enough electrolytes, and it ended in disastrous leg cramps.

Then there was the racecourse itself. It contained twelve solid miles of hills. Even after a relatively flat segment at the beginning, the hills kept coming. As a runner, you don't ever get to coast — or let up — your feet are in motion for the entire distance. I suspect that is why Pheidippides died running that first marathon.

Under the starting line banner, there were runners everywhere looking confident, stretching, jogging in place, checking their shoes laces, and waiting for the satellite to connect with their Garmin sports watch. For the moment, my prostate biopsy, my job search, and

Photo by: David Johndrow

October 27, 2013
This is it, the starting line of the Cape Cod Marathon. 938 days since I had been confined to a bed in the I.C.U., and there are two minutes until the starting cannon would sound.

DAVID JOHNDROW

whatever the next day might have held, were far from my mind.

Ahead of me lay the loftiest goal I had ever tried to achieve.

At 8:28, a jazz performer sang an acappella rendition of "America the Beautiful" which rang out into the cool fall air. The sun was just peeking over the buildings on Main Street as I stood with my hand over my heart. For the moment, I felt proud to be an American, and part of a marathon. These patriotic songs seemed to be more meaningful since the Boston Marathon bombings.

The starting cannon boomed and the first of over 1000 runners moved across the starting line. I switched on my GPS watch and tucked my iPhone into the arm holder. Crossing the timing mat, I high-fived my friend Tom Frazier who was working as a volunteer on the course. Tommy and I have known each other for over a decade. He's an accomplished marathoner. He also enjoys reminding me of the days when I was fat, as we talk about running for hours.

As a game-time decision I chose to use Jeff Galloway's walk/run method. Instead of running continuously, you simply run for three minutes and then walk one minute to recover. It is sounds slow, but many runners actually have better overall times by only running 75% of the race. Using this method you run nearly twenty miles of the marathon and walk about seven. Many novice marathoners end up walking much of the last five or six miles because their bodies become laden with muscle cramping lactic acid. I decided to run the length of Main Street before doing any walks to enjoy the energy of the crowd.

As the pack turned towards the harbor, it was time for my first walk. Looking around, I saw nearly a dozen walkers. I looked at one fellow, "run/walk?" I asked.

"Absolutely!" was his emphatic reply.

"Me too," came a woman's voice from the other side of the street.

"What are your intervals?" I asked.

"Two run and one walk," was her reply.

I looked at my Garmin and it was time to run again. I took off and they followed. Three minutes later I shuffled to a walk. Another sixty seconds passed and I ran some more.

Walking gives you an opportunity to look around, and the

Falmouth Inner Harbor is quite beautiful. I came to my senses as the crowds thinned to an occasional cluster of townsfolk sitting on the porch having their morning caffeine brew. The excitement died down, and now it was time to draw on my own strength, so I prayed. The course rounded a corner on the other side of the harbor and then up a hill. I thought, this is an easy one, as I took advantage of the down side heading onto a long flat beach portion of the course.

I lost track of my running and walking as I ran. I slowed to get back on pace. This is a lot of discipline I thought, but I knew it would pay off in the end. I thought about fighter pilots throttling it back to conserve fuel so they could return from a mission. Of course, I did have a little fun along the way. There were water and Gatorade stops every three miles. "Where's the beer?" I teased the volunteers, as I grabbed one cup of water and one Gatorade, mixing them together because straight Gatorade makes my mouth dry.

I proceeded down the road in a brisk walk, gulping my future fuel. The human body is not like a car, it needs fuel twenty or more minutes before it needs to use it. It is interesting, that the body can manage to process oxygen for about an hour during a run. At that point, a runner can no longer keep up with the demand for oxygen while simultaneously ridding itself of the waste. It miraculously switches over to another fuel source called glycogen. One of the reasons runners eat a lot of carbs in the days before, is to make sure these stores are as full as humanly possible. The body is even more efficient. When runners hit "the wall", it is usually about twenty miles into a race. For me it was twenty-two. That was most likely because of the walk/run intervals. The body makes a last ditch effort and begins to burn fat. This is why a runner can get past the wall, and finish the last grueling 6.2 miles.

I am not a doctor (though I'd like to play one on TV), and of course there is some dispute on how and why all this physiology actually works, but that is a simplistic view of a very complex process. What I did know, is that thousands of runners finish marathons each year, so it works, *somehow* it works.

My focus changed from the beautiful scenery to a very low flying Massachusetts State Police helicopter, which circled very close to the course pulling heavily to one side. It was like a scene out of an action film. I could even see an intense "cop-like" expression on the pilot's face. I had a moment where I thought about Boston — some extra vigilance, just to be safe. They abruptly turned and went back off in the other direction. I looked out over the water, and lost track of my run/walk ratio again. Mile four was my fastest mile of the race, and at a 10:16 pace, it was too fast.

Passing another group of spectators in their front yards, there was a man with a pot of coffee refilling mugs for our cheering section. "Is this the coffee stop?" I asked. They laughed and cheered me on holding their mugs high. Their neighbors looked like they were a little uncertain what all the noise was about. One gentleman with morning head, stood bleary-eyed in his pajamas with his mouth hanging open.

As the time and the miles passed by a group of timeshare hotels, I checked my Garmin watch. 11:10 per mile, the perfect pace! I had worked in the corporate office of one of the hotel chains along that beautiful stretch of waterfront. I looked out over the beach where my young daughter, Charlotte, had picked up her first seashell. Then I looked down the row of numbered doors to locate the suite my wife and I had spent our first anniversary in. I smiled as I thought about having used the door latch to open a bottle of sparkling cider for our celebration that night.

I settled in with a group of run/walkers and a couple of self-proclaimed "slow" runners. One woman was doing fifty marathons in fifty states before she turned fifty; this was number seventeen. Mather just did this race each year because of the beautiful course and the time of year. I met a father-daughter team, too. They had done a thirty mile run/walk training run together to get ready!

Nine miles had rolled by with a bajillion thoughts orbiting my one busy brain cell. Then, before me, was the first *real* hill. I had already planned to walk up it, so I rolled it back to an easy walk. I was ahead of schedule anyway. I desperately needed to save something for the end of the race. John's watch beeped off his run/walk strategy. If they could do thirty miles, they should be able to finish 26.2. I stuck with them.

I passed spectators holding signs of encouragement. "Go Stranger Go!", "Toenails are for sissies!", "Free Beer and Sex at the Finish!" (marriage is wonderful), and "You Rock Mom!"

"I wish I was a mom." I said as I passed by.

There were a couple of good downhills, and I did my own thing. The dynamic duo caught back up with me on my next walk break. We chatted a little about Cape Cod during our minute breaks. I also walked the water stops where I mixed my Gatorade and water cocktails. I had brought two pockets full of snacks. As I got hungry, I ate dried cranberries, granola bars, and pretzels. Replenishing salt and water is very important during a race like this, and the sugar in the cranberries gave me a little boost.

Crossing the half-marathon mark (13.1 miles), the clock read two hours and twenty-eight minutes. It was reasonably close to both of my two disastrous hot and humid half-marathons that I did in the weeks prior. I guess I was a little surprised that I didn't feel badly at all. I tried not to think about those other races, and focused on the "now". I felt fine. My legs felt good, my rhythm was comfortable, and all my joints seemed to be holding up to the pounding. I took a minute to savor this gorgeous fall day on Cape Cod. It could not have been better running weather!

And run I did.

Down across a recently-harvested cranberry bog, our little pack of brightly-colored sojourners went. I slowed to a walk, as prescribed by my watch. There were a couple of other walkers, and I chatted it up with a nurse from New York, and a Norwegian national living in the States. Checking my watch, I said "good luck" to the ladies and took off down the road for another three-minute blast.

The race volunteers had stopped traffic at a busy intersection as a couple of dozen marathoners began to cross. All of a sudden there was a commotion as a driver tried to pull out onto the course. He was swearing at the volunteer holding a stop/go sign. "Go ahead and call the cops", the volunteer said in a respectful, but forceful voice. More swearing ensued as the SUV made its way onto the course, crowding the runners at the intersection.

"Call the police on that idiot in the blue Mercedes." I said to the next three or four volunteers, as I motioned behind me.

A moment or two later, I came across a police officer at another intersection. "Can you arrest that jerk in the blue Mercedes back there?" I said as I motioned by tipping my head back.

He laughed, "Did you want me to shoot him too?"

"Twice in the head, thank you!"

I ran on.

From the course elevations I saw online, I had only been concerned about the two miles of hills between miles nine and eleven. Having traversed those with ease, I would have relaxed a little, thinking the worst was over. However, my friend Tommy had driven the course with me the day before and got a good look at what lay ahead: the Sippewissett Hills. It was five miles of rolling sand dunes. No one hill was difficult by itself; it was simply the fact that there were dozens and dozens of them. I decided to change my strategy. I was going to walk uphill to conserve energy and run downhill to make up some time and forget the watch.

As I passed a little store in the village, there was a small crowd of spectators. I heard one them ask someone they were with, "can you drink wine this early in the morning?"

"Yes!" I said, as I passed by, joining the conversation.

"The perfect morning", one of them replied.

Up the hills and down the hills I went — running, walking, snacking, praying, and listening to Endomondo on my iPhone chirp out my heart rate and average pace. "Eighteen miles, heart rate 151 beats per minute, average pace: 11:23", said the electronic female voice.

"Thank you, Jesus!" was all that I could think to say, and so I did. Although eighteen miles was my best long run of the summer, it was still a tough one because it rained cats and dogs for two solid hours that day. I had some pretty bad chafing, too.

There was a runner ahead with a "Boston Strong" shirt on. We walked a hill together. In a heavy foreign accent, he said, "I call you endorphin. I like you shirt says 'If it were not for the endorphins, I would still be on the couch.'"

I smiled, "did you run Boston?"

"Yes, I do no finish — bombs, you know", he said as we walked a little farther. It made me glad for all the state and local police along with some officers from the sheriff's department that were so visible all along the race route that day. We took off running again.

My walk/runs seemed to have me passing him, and him passing me, for the next few miles. Each time he would pass me, he'd say, "bye bye, endorphin." When I would pass him, with a little laugh, he would say, "There go endorphin".

I met a couple of ladies, Jenny and Christina, Christina was doing her first marathon, too. We walked and ran through the golf course, and I bade them farewell on the next long downhill.

The next water stop was sponsored by members of the U.S. military who were stationed nearby at the Otis Air National Guard base. There was lot of camo, American flags, and trick-or-treat candy! God bless our troops. Thank you God, for fun-size Twix and Snickers too!

I walked to the water stop and met a guy around my age. He wore a shirt on the back of which said, "In Memory of Sarah" with a photo of a little girl about my daughter's age. "What's Sarah's story?" I asked.

He seemed slightly surprised and replied with tears coming to his eyes, "she was my little girl, and died of a traumatic brain injury while sledding this past winter."

"I am so sorry for your loss." It was all I could say. I just wished I had something better to say. He thanked me, shook my hand, and I started my next run interval. At the next intersection there were three women with babies in infant carriers. "Is this the baby stop?" I asked. They laughed and gave me a high-five.

I clicked off mile nineteen.

I didn't see too many runners through the mile twenty marker. Passing Quissett Harbor, I had a little cry (okay, a big one) as I broke the barrier. It was the longest distance I had ever run in my life. On the side of the road a short time later, there was another State Trooper on a motorcycle. "Can I borrow the keys for twenty minutes?" I said.

He replied with a little laugh, "they don't need keys!"

I kept on running.

Late in the race there were no crowds, just a few race marshals every half mile or so. I thanked them for being out there. The salt was forming on my skin like fine beach sand. My calves were tight, so I slowed to a walk and tried to stretch them out.

I was considering my final run. It's just a 10K I have left. Even a bad time would make it seventy minutes, I thought. I had been running for three hours and forty-five minutes. I am going to be under five hours — the thought made me happy. I pressed on, but decided to still take the walk breaks. I had no idea what the next six or so miles would bring, so I stuck with the program.

I pressed on through the village of Woods Hole, up the hill past the harbor, and heading out of town. Up another hill and then a right turn on Church Street as the course made its way to the beach. I passed a runner who looked to be about my age on the next incline. "Looking good", I said as pulled up alongside him.

"I'm Mike", he said between exhales.

"I'm David, have a good race", and I ran off. We passed each other a few more times as I stuck with my run/walk strategy.

"You're like a truck. I pass you on the uphills and you pass me on the downhills", Mike said.

I smiled and started my next three-minute run.

There was a long straightaway past the beach and I decided to run the entire length. It was beautiful, a slight breeze, sunshine and just a few miles left. I felt good, but the calves were feeling the burn as I rounded the hill at Nobska Lighthouse. Then, I saw the woman I chatted with at the starting line. "Hey!" I shouted as I passed her. She was stepping out of a race support van. I didn't slow to see what the problem was.

"Good luck!" she yelled back.

Up the hills walking, and down the hills running, mile twenty-three came and went. Just 5K left to go.

I had run a hundred 5Ks in the last year. It was my go-to distance on an easy day – just 3.1 miles. I've got this, I thought to myself. Four hours and twenty minutes had passed. I have forty minutes to finish this race, and my worst time ever was thirty-two minutes. I shed a few tears; this marathon was mine. Thank you, Lord, I said quietly as I grabbed that last of my granola bar on a walk break.

I had been alone for some time at that point. My skin was covered in dried salt, and my legs were getting heavier, and my calves were stiff. My heart rate was fine and my pace was good. Suddenly I heard, "Endorphin! You still running?", Boston passed me with a slow jog and smile.

In the distance I could hear music. I was now running with Vince, a cancer survivor from Vermont. "It sounds like Heaven"

I said, hoping it was a water stop. As we rounded the bend, there in the middle of the road, was Elvis! "We *are* in Heaven, Vince!" The King was handing out trick-or-treat candy to the weary along with cool drinks. "Thank you very much" I said in my best Memphis drawl.

Vince and I pressed on - running three, walking one.

The "Tired Runner" vehicle was making its way in the other direction circling to find those who just couldn't finish the race. They offered a cool bottle of water out the window. "Thank you; it's the next best thing to a ride", I said.

"We've got those too", the driver quipped.

"If I have to crawl, I am finishing this race!" I fired back.

October 27, 2013
The dream realized — the finish line of the Cape Cod Marathon.

Down along the beach I had a Charlie Horse (leg cramp) that was so bad I nearly fell in the sand along the side of the beach road. Vince helped me along, he was hurting, too. We walked it off and ran another few hundred yards when the cramps started again. On and off they came. I rallied another run and took off with less than a mile to go.

They hit again. I stopped and steadied myself against a telephone pole.

Vince caught back up to

me. We ran a few hundred feet and walked a few hundred. Just before the left turn onto Main Street, Vince was sagging behind. I yelled at him, "Come on buddy, the race has just begun!"

Then I turned and gave it everything I had for the last few hundred yards.

They called my name out on the P.A., "here comes David Johndrow of Uxbridge, Massachusetts."

I didn't care about the clock or the fanfare any longer, I just wanted to finish and rest my legs.

I crossed the finish line and the volunteers met me with water, a finisher's medal, and a space blanket. From the crowd, an old co-worker came up to congratulate me. Then I turned and saw Vince limping across the finish line.

"You got this!" I yelled to him.

I leaned against a water table and stretched my calves a bit. I tried to pose for a picture my friend offered to take. I turned around to see Mike meet his wife at the finish. He came over to shake my hand, and his wife gave me a hug. They were overjoyed at his finish. I don't know his story, but I know there was one.

My legs were on fire as I steadied myself on a crowd barrier. My friend Marcia was crying, "You made it — how incredible!"

"I did it. I made it all the way from the I.C.U. to the finish line of a marathon."

Praise the Lord.

end?

Recipes Even Lazy People Can Make

Apple and Banana Parfait
1 sliced Granny Smith or other favorite apple
1 sliced banana
1/4 cup of shelled walnuts
1/4 cup of dried cranberries
1/2 cup of Greek Yogurt 0% plain

Black Bean Chili
1 can of black beans rinsed
1 large can of "no salt added" crushed tomatoes
½ cup of sliced raw or sautéed onions
1 pinch of chili powder
¼ - ½ cup of your favorite salsa
1 small can of corn is optional

Bacon Wrapped Water Chestnuts
1 pound of nitrate free or low-sodium bacon
2 small cans of whole water chestnuts
Toothpicks
Chili sauce optional

Avocado Salad
1 Haas avocado sliced
1 vine ripened tomato
½ cup of lower sodium cottage cheese or Greek yogurt and humus
1 teaspoon of lemon or lime juice
A dash of cracked pepper or hot sauce
A sprinkle of grated cheese optional

Eggs in a Muffin Tin

Olive Oil

1 Dozen Eggs

Salmon

Salsa

Swiss Cheese

Turkey Sausage Patties

Bacon

Tomato slices

Spinach

Feta

Spray or brush on olive oil in each muffin holder.

Crack an egg or add scramble egg mixture

Top with sausage patty, bacon, salmon, spinach, tomato &
feta, or salsa and cheese

Bake at 350 for about 35 minutes.

Freeze and microwave to reheat

Acknowledgments

Art direction, layout and design by Bob Pierce Design, Milton, Vermont, bobandstephie@comcast.net

Friend, fellow coffee drinker, proofreader, encourager, and phrase coiner, Rev. Bobby Daniel

Video and video production, Dan Dillavou

Nutritionist and fact checker,
Dr. Coreyann Poly, PhD, RDN, CDE
CEO Dieticians of New England
www.donediet.org   experts@donediet.org

Long time friend, photographer, and race support vehicle driver, Scott White

Long time friend and marathoner wisdom possessor, Cindy White

The running machine and training analyst, Carson Williams

Grammar Guru, Andrea B. Ortiz, M.Ed.
andreabrianne@gmail.com

Google fact finder, Angie Nichols
trumpelope@hotmail.com

Creative input, lifelong friend, Percy Tierney

My run club family, Tri-Valley Frontrunners
www.tri-valleyfrontrunners.com

The smartest idiots I know on Facebook, Idiots Running Club

One of my favorite Facebook groups, Run Junkees

A great community of supporters: My Fitness Pal
www.myfitnesspal.com

My favorite running store, PR Running in Westborough, MA
www.myprrun.com

One of my favorite smartphone Apps, encouragers, and awesome
people: Noom
www.noom.com

One of my sponsors, Larry Osborn of Runners ID
www.runnersid.com

Donors

Amanda Cody	Dee Ann Hill
Amoreena Schindler	Deidre Akins
Amy Zollner	Denise Jones
Andrew Archer	Diana Guzman
Andrew Tucker	Dottie Courtney Hansen
Angela Murray	Elaine Neill
Angelia Twitty Howard	Eliz George
Anne Jacobs Velazquez	Elizabeth Nonn
Anthony Cradic	Ellen Hasbrouck
Barney Wynne	Faith Raymond
BC Atkinson	Georgia
Benjamin B. Ford	Ginny Ernest-Taylor
Beth Sandahl	Greg Palmer
Bill Campbell	Gwen Bernardy
Bob Brown	Heidi Anne Welch
Bobby Daniel	Holly
Carolann Slayton	Hunter Malin
Cathy Jones	Inky
Charles Saari	Jacob Coonradt
Cherie Frank	Jamie Jackson
Cherilynn Blumenthal	Janet Brunsilius
Chou Campbell	Jasmine Oravec
Chrissandra Porter	Jason Kasper
Christine Lesmerises	Jen Weddington
Craig Hubachek	Jennifer McLaughlin
Dana Dillavou	Jenny Newbury
Daniel Egenlauf	Jim Marrs
Darcy Boyer	John Sotirkys
David Dumas	John Whitnet
David Salvas	Jon Comtois
Deana Runyon	Joyce Johannesen

Karen Dodos
Kathryn Walby
Kathy Ford
Ken Webb
Kevin Lynch
Kim Willis
Kris Fink
Kristie Barlow
Laurie Greenwood
Leah Goldstein
Leslie Swart LMT
Linda Lou
Lisa Schultz
Little Laura
Liz Johndrow
Marcia MacInnis
Marian Murphy
Marjorie Downey
Marjorie Michelle Francis
Martha and Steve Heassler
Mary Dimoglis Regula
Mary Jane Choachuy
Matt Appling
Matthew Philip Wee
Maureen Celmer
Meghan Godbey
Melissa Graham
Merrick Finn
Michael Garone
Michael Potorti
Michael Skillin
Michele Coia-Veston
Michelle Marshall
Michelle Snyder
Mione Haak
Monica Aldridge
Mrs S Geer
Nancy Dunphy Wilson
Nicole Barnabe

Noelle Noonan
Pamela Goloskie
Patricia Corey-Lisle
Paula Aishe
Paula Strauss
Peggy Haynes
Percy Tierney
Regina Esposito Allegra
Renee Ciszek
Rhonda Miller Smith
Rich Bigelow
Rina Martin
Rob Whall
Roc Vernen
Ross D. Jones
S Ray Constantine
Sally Fairchild Wykes
Samantha Nottingham
Samantha Richardson
Sandra Masiello
Scot Motyka
Scott White
Shana King
Sharon Markwardt
Sherene
Sherry Conklin
Stephan Kraus
Steve Burgess
Steven Ktenas
Sue Crusen
Suzanne Raffalli
Teresa Talley
Theresa Lehman
Time2LoseWeightNow
Todd Hickey
Tom Frost
Trish C
Valerie Wolford
Vladimir Vukicevic

David Johndrow

The Man, The Action Hero, The Legend — The Survivor

Photo by: Sarah J. Thornington-Cericola, The Studio by The Sea (www.thestudiobythesea.com)

I've known David since we grew up in southern Connecticut back in the dark ages (the 70s), each of us graduating from North Branford High School in 1975 and 1976, respectively. Though we have a lot in common, in that our lives seem to have followed similar paths, we have some distinct differences. For example, David is a caffeine junkie, not emerging from his morning coma until his third cup of coffee. I have a Diet Dr. Pepper in the morning and drink water all day. David loves sushi, I call it "bait". But one thing that we have in common is that we both love the Lord, have given our lives to Jesus, and I am honored that he has asked me to help him with this book, including writing this biography.

David was born at the trailing edge of the post-WWII baby boom and grew up in the bedroom community of Northford, which was actually the northern borough of the town of North Branford, but with its own schools, post office, churches, and retail center (coupled with the fact that our town was bisected north-and-south by a large lake and a quarry), for all practical purposes, Northford was its own town. Together we dreamed of eventually having our own McDonald's restaurant.

This little slice of suburbia was still rife with open land, woods, and sand-pits where we all grew up playing outside, building tree forts, joining a friendly game of baseball in the streets, and riding our dirt bikes. Home computers and handheld game gizmos didn't exist yet, but we found ways to amuse ourselves without getting into too much trouble in the vast amusement park our parents called "outside".

In high school, David was a part of our inaugural hockey team (go Thunderbirds!), and continues his passion for the game to this day by playing in local amateur leagues. Active in all sorts of outdoor sports, he also played guitar just as frenetically, jamming with friends in their suburban garage bands.

David continued his education by studying music at the University of Hartford's Hart School of Music, and art at the Portland School of Art. More recently, he's added to his higher education with studies in computer science at Stanford University.

Since high school, his life has been a roller-coaster. One of the biggest dragons that he's had to slay was that of alcoholism. Sober for thirty years, the next dragon to slay was heart disease. As you read this book, you'll see the details of just how, through some unexpected circumstances, he ended up in the intensive-care unit with talk of heart transplants and his amazing recovery borne of sheer determination and faith.

Along the journey of his life, he encountered Christ, and surrendered his life to Him, and that faith has been an integral part of this story. In fact, after his pastor had visited him in the hospital and shared some encouraging words, David dreamed of running again, and began his "training" by walking around the cardio ward, pushing his I.V. stand along with him, before he was even discharged.

In those ensuing years between high school and today, he has had three daughters, two of which are now grown and on their own, the third is still a pre-teen as I write this, and still living at home (the apple of her daddy's eye), with his beautiful and supportive wife, Mary Anne. The family lived together for over twenty years on Cape Cod, where David also worked.

Today, they live in a small rural town in south-central Massachusetts, which boasts two traffic lights (one on either side of the same intersection), and a small commercial building in the center of town that is shared by both a local bank and a gun shop. A far cry from the wilds of city life!

A husband, father, world-traveller, and self-admitted guitar-shredding software geek, he has added to that list of adjectives — by necessity — runner, marathoner, amateur nutritionist, and all-around health nerd. And, in wanting to share his experiences with the world, writer.

Now in his fifties, he has turned much of his creative effort to writing, and helping to inspire others who have suddenly, after blissfully-ignorant years of deteriorating heath and expanding belt-lines, realized the unhealthy situations they have found themselves in. Hoping to inspire them to get up off their couches and make some drastic lifestyle changes because, hey, if a fat, junk-food scarfing, heart attack survivor from Connecticut can do it, then anyone can do it.

The biggest danger in reading David's book, is that you will no longer have any excuses — and that can only be a good thing.

It's your future, start living it now.

— *Bob Pierce*

Glossary

Runner Buzzwords for Cocktail Parties

If you have not been a runner, or you are new to it, here's some runner's jargon you might find helpful. If not, I think you'll still find it amusing, that's why you bought the book!

Achilles Tendon: Any tendon that hurts from running.

Aerobic: So out of breath that you wish you were dead.

Anaerobic: Aerobic's kid sister.

Bandit: Runs a race without a number on.

Bathroom: These are usually porta-potties - with the emphasis on potty! Bring your own hand sanitizer, and possibly a tazer.

Bib: Keeps snot rockets (nasal effluvia) off of a runner's tech-t, and can be used for a lobster dinner.

Black Toenail (Runner's toe): 1. Goth runner gear. 2. Caused by shoes that are too small.

Bloody Nipples: 1. Tomato juice with 2 shots of tequila. 2. Just one more thing that men use to gross out women. 3. Hot shower alarm.

Carb-loading: Drinking beer and eating pizza.

Chip: 1. Made of chocolate and the reason you need MFP. 2. Embedded in your number by big brother and the race officials.

Chip Time: The time your chip crossed the finish line. If it is on your person, it's good. If it's in an ambulance, it's not so good.

Cool Down: Sudden drop in temperature after guzzling a cold beer or other suitable beverage after a race.

Corral: A place to keep nervous runners before the race.

Dedication: Too much fiber the day before a race.

DNF: Did Not Finish. Better than **DNS:** Did Not Start.

Drafting: 1. Beer after the race. 2. Running closely behind other runners to avoid the head wind.

Endorphins: *sigh* the runner's significant other.

Elite Runner: Faster than humanly possible!

Fartlek: 1. A winning strategy when others are drafting you. 2. Swedish for speed play.

Gun Time: 1. An expression used in place of "the straw that broke the camel's back." 2. It is especially useful with annoying people.

Hitting the Wall: Mad because you can't find your running shoes, or forgot to start your Garmin.

Intervals: Taking turns watching the kids so you can get a workout in.

Jog: Remembering your name at the registration table.

Minimalism: Rogue religion. The terrorists of the running world.

Negative Splits: 1. Wearing embarrassingly tight clothing and bending over to tie your shoe. 2. Running the last half of a race faster.

Pace: The speed at which you actually can run.

Passing: *verb* 1. Gas 2. mile/kilometer markers 3. Other runners

Pick-Ups: 1. Asking for phone numbers and Facebook names at the start line. 2. Running fast spurts.

Pronation: 1. Patriotism. 2. Nerd term for foot strike.

Race: The obligation to do what you think you can't.

Runner's High: If you run, you know.

Safety Pins: Not as safe as they claim to be, but used for attaching race bibs.

Side Stitch: Used by runners who knit.

Sneakers: Cheap running shoes.

Stinky Feet: Stinky feet.

Supination: A small super power.

Target Heart Rate: Anything greater than let's say 10 beats per hour.

Ten Percent Rule: Runners who spend one tenth of their income on race fees.

Toe Box: What they put your toes into to be cremated.

Ultra: Running the day away.

VO2 max: Canadian whisky.

Walking: Plum tuckered out, but not a bad thing.

Wall (The): A place where wailing happens a lot.

Winning: 1. What Charlie Sheen thinks he does. 2. What you will be if you just sign up for a race.

Bibliography

Apples and More / University of Illinois Extension
http://urbanext.illinois.edu/apples/nutrition.cfm

Avocado Nutrition Information
http://www.californiaavocado.com/nutrition/

Beans: Protein-Rich Superfoods by Jenny Stamos Kovacs for WebMD the Magazine
http://www.webmd.com/diet/features/beans-protein-rich-superfoods

Blueberry Crisp, Vegan and Gluten Free
http://healthymamainfo.com/2012/07/blueberry-crisp-vegan-gluten-free/

It's All Better with Broccoli
http://www.superfoodsrx.com/superfoods/broccoli/its-all-better-with-broccoli.html

The World's Healthiest Foods
http://www.whfoods.com/genpage.php?tname=foodspice&dbid=9

20 Health Benefits of Cinnamon
http://cinnamonvogue.com/cinnamoncommonuses.html

The Nutrition of Dark Chocolate
http://www.fitday.com/fitness-articles/nutrition/healthy-eating/the-nutrition-of-dark-chocolate.html

12 Healthiest Dried Fruits
http://www.fitday.com/fitness-articles/nutrition/healthy-eating/12-healthiest-dried-fruits.html

Olive Oil Health Benefits
http://www.oliveoiltimes.com/olive-oil-health-benefits

Unlocking the Benefits of Garlic by Tara Parker-Pope for The NY Times
http://well.blogs.nytimes.com/2007/10/15/unlocking-the-benefits-of-garlic/?_r=0

The World's Healthiest Foods
http://www.whfoods.com/genpage.php?tname=foodspice&dbid=96

Greek Yogurt Vs. Regular Yogurt: Which is More Healthful? By Angela Haupt for USNews
http://health.usnews.com/health-news/diet-fitness/diet/articles/2011/09/30/greek-yogurt-vs-regular-yogurt-which-is-more-healthful

The World's Healthiest Foods
http://www.whfoods.com/genpage.php?tname=foodspice&dbid=66

An Onion a Day?
http://www.sweetonionsource.com/healthy.html

The World's Healthiest Foods
http://www.whfoods.com/genpage.php?tname=foodspice&dbid=37

Doctor Warns: Eat Soy and You'll Look 5 Years Older by Dr. Mercola
http://articles.mercola.com/sites/articles/archive/2011/12/08/the-dirty-little-secret-hidden-in-much-of-your-health-food.aspx

The Nutrient Value of White Potatoes vs. Sweet Potatoes by Louise Tremblay for SFGate
http://healthyeating.sfgate.com/nutrient-value-white-potatoes-vs-sweet-potatoes-4221.html

Healthy Super Foods
http://www.naturalhealingcare.com/healthy-super-foods/

How Food Affects Osteoporosis
http://www.joybauer.com/osteoporosis/how-food-affects-osteoporosis.aspx

Health Benefits by Function & Organ
http://theteaspot.com/tea-health-benefits-functions.html

Lycopene Benefits
http://lycopenebenefits.org/

The World's Healthiest Foods
http://www.whfoods.com/genpage.php?tname=foodspice&dbid=44

Why is Turkey Better than Chicken?
http://www.weightlossforall.com/why-is-turkey-better-than-chicken.htm

Health Benefits of Nuts and Seeds
http://www.joybauer.com/food-articles/nuts-and-seeds.aspx

Fiftysomething Diet: 5 Powerful Weight-Loss Boosters by Maureen Callahan for Huffington Post
http://www.huffingtonpost.com/2013/03/28/how-to-lose-weight_n_2965765.html

Simply Asparagus
http://juicerecipes.com/recipes/simply-asparagus-3

The Top 10 Aphrodisiac Foods by Sanela for Session Magazine
http://www.alternet.org/story/132846/the_top_10_aphrodisiac_foods

10 Foods that Boost Your Libido (and 3 that Kill It) by FITNESS Magazine
http://shine.yahoo.com/healthy-living/10-foods-boost-libido-3-kill-172700706.html

Amino Acids
http://menssexualhealthinfo.wordpress.com/amino-acids/

25 Foods that Are Natural Aphrodisiacs
http://kimberlysnyder.net/blog/2011/10/03/25-foods-that-are-natural-aphrodisiacs/

10 Foods That Sound Healthy (but Aren't) by Katherine Brooking for Cooking Light
http://www.cookinglight.com/eating-smart/smart-choices/top-10-unhealthy-foods-00400000054971/page13.html

Runner's World Training Guide
http://www.runnersworld.com/sites/default/files/NutritionGuide_0.pdf

The World's Healthiest Foods
http://www.whfoods.com/genpage.php?tname=george&dbid=24

Artificial Sweeteners and Other Sugar Substitutes
http://www.mayoclinic.com/health/artificial-sweeteners/MY00073

Chickopedia: What Consumers Need to Know
http://www.nationalchickencouncil.org/about-the-industry/chickopedia/

How Food Affects High Triglycerides
http://www.joybauer.com/high-triglycerides/about-high-triglycerides.aspx

Grass-Fed Beef versus Grain-Fed Beef
http://www.cookinglight.com/cooking-101/resources/grass-fed-beef-grain-fed-beef-00412000070712/page2.html

DAVID JOHNDROW

28305222R00119

Made in the USA
Charleston, SC
07 April 2014